# THE FOUR SEASONS
# OF T'ANG POETRY

# THE
# FOUR SEASONS
## OF
# T'ANG POETRY

BY

JOHN C. H. WU

CHARLES E. TUTTLE COMPANY

RUTLAND, VERMONT          TOKYO, JAPAN

REPRESENTATIVES
Continental Europe: BOXERBOOKS, INC., Zurich
British Isles: PRENTICE-HALL INTERNATIONAL, INC., London
Australasia: PAUL FLESCH & CO., PTY. LTD., Melbourne
Canada: M. G. HURTING LTD., Edmonton

*Published by the Charles E. Tuttle Company, Inc.
of Rutland, Vermont & Tokyo, Japan
with editorial offices at
2-6, Suido 1-chome, Bunkyo-ku, Tokyo, Japan (112)*

73-8950

*Library of Congress Catalog Card No. 71-171997
International Standard Book No. 0-8048-0197-5*

PRINTED IN JAPAN

TO MY WIFE AGNES CHUK WU
WHO—GOD HELPING—
HAS TURNED THE WINTER OF MY LIFE
INTO SPRING

# CONTENTS

# ILLUSTRATIONS

*Courtesy of*
*The National Palace Museum, Taiwan, Republic of China*

# PROLOGUE

## By WILLIAM G. GODDARD*

IT HAS BEEN SAID that in the life of man on this planet there have been three perfect moments—T'ang poetry, Sung painting, and Ming porcelain.

Be this as it may, it cannot be denied that in the poetry of T'ang we hear the music of souls as close to the divine in Nature as it has ever been given to mortals to attain.

It is this music-in-poetry, attuned to the seasons of life, with which the following pages deal.

When I was asked by the author to write this prologue I hesitated. I felt that a work of such quality merited a worthier pen than mine, certainly one more competent. However, if a keen appreciation of John C. H. Wu's literary efforts over many years together with a more than superficial knowledge of Chinese literature will be accepted as justification for writing this introduction, I can proceed, confident that the high standard of the following pages will make up for any deficiency on my part.

Over the years since Western sinologues turned to the study of

* Dr. William G. Goddard is an Australian Sinologist whose works are well known in the Republic of China, the United States, Australia, and England, where he now makes his home. He has lectured widely and has had seven books published, including one written in the Chinese language. His latest work is entitled *Formosa: A Study in Chinese History*. He established and served as the first Director of the Institute of Pacific Studies at the China Academy in Taiwan, to which he was elected as a Fellow in 1969.

Chinese poetry, many translations of T'ang poems have appeared, some good, some indifferent, and others without much relevance to the Chinese texts. It is one thing to render a Chinese character correctly, that is, in terms of the lexicon, but to sense what the poet felt when he brushed his characters is quite a different matter. Possibly, this is because few Western translators have possessed that sensitivity to the spiritual in Nature, which is the very soul of Chinese poetry. C. P. Hsu must have had this in mind when he wrote:

*Strictly speaking, poetry is untranslatable: it is to be felt. But since we do translate poetry, we must consider it an art, which requires something more than mere technique. A good translator should understand the poet and the poem he is translating so well that he himself becomes imbued with the spirit of the poem.*

Few Western translators of T'ang poetry have moved beyond the possession of the technique to the attainment of the art.

One Chinese critic, after paying tribute to Arthur Waley's translations, which "grasped the essence of Chinese poetry," contends that some of these are "not free from mistakes," while Herbert Giles, meticulous as he was in the matter of meter and rhyme, was often "obliged to prefer inversions to clearness and simplicity, which are the highest standard of art, especially in literature." Witter Bynner attempted to overcome the difficulty by co-operating with the Chinese scholar Kiang Kang-hu, but here, again, the music of the T'ang poems was lost. Perhaps, the wide gulf between the Chinese and Western languages made this inevitable.

In the following pages, we have, I believe, the most successful attempt, so far, not only to enable the reader to feel what the T'ang poet felt, but also, to some extent, to hear the music of the poem. If not the complete score, at least some of the interpretive notes. Echoes from the hills of Shensi.

In John C. H. Wu, two worlds have become one. Not only does he, being himself Chinese, sense the inner soul of the poet and feel his meaning, but is able, also, to express this in the most appropriate English form. Not one pulsing of the spirit of the T'ang poet is lost for want of the correct English word.

John C. H. Wu is not the only son of Asia who has succeeded in living in two worlds, intellectually and spiritually. At the moment, I think of Gregorio Zaide, who introduced his study of Philippine culture in these words:

*Only a Filipino—with the blood of Mother Asia and the soul of Malaysia—can really feel with sympathetic understanding the heartbeats of the Filipino people and interpret faithfully their impulses, idiosyncracies, customs, and traditions. Indeed, only a Filipino—steeped in the lore and folkways of his own people and enlightened by the progressive arts and sciences of the Western world—can portray fairly the trials and tribulations of his compatriots and express with resonant poignancy their ideals and aspirations and dreams during the changing eras of their history.*

As we turn the following pages, we seem to be looking through a spiritual kaleidoscope and seeing mortals, just like ourselves, struggling with the immortal issues of life and the universe. That they lived centuries before our time makes no difference. Some are deep in thought, some cry, some shout for joy, while others just abandon the quest for an answer in bleak despair.

At one extreme, we see Wang Wei, standing as a seer on some promontory of the spirit, surveying the scene; then, far below, on the plain, Li Po, as though in futile jest, invites us to accept, with him, the gospel of the grape. And between these two, spiritually, are others, a great company, each with his own problem, his own attachment, and in some cases, his own sorrow, even though it be for a fallen leaf in autumn.

So it is that the seasons of T'ang poetry become also the seasons of the soul of universal man.

This interpretation by the author is a remarkable achievement; yet not more unusual than the author himself. To understand the following pages, we must know something of the man who wrote them. That is, insofar as it is possible to psychoanalyze a personality. We can understand the tools a craftsman brings with him to his task, even when this is translating a T'ang poem, but only to a limited degree can we comprehend the inner experience that guides him in his interpretation. However, in this case, that little will help us.

Professionally, the author of the following pages is a lawyer and in that sphere enjoys a distinguished record. At one time, he was Chief Justice of the Provisional Court of Shanghai and later played an important part in framing the Constitution of the Republic of China. Till recently, he was professor of law at Seton Hall University in the United States. His books and articles on legal subjects have been published in Chinese, English, French and German.

But, together with this, and herein lies his uniqueness, he is a poet. More than that, a mystic poet. Perhaps, this is the result of his earlier Buddhist training before he embraced Christianity. John C. H. Wu would have been a most inviting study for Sigmund Freud, who would, doubtless, have found the Wu mysticism a Christo-Buddhist mood. There is, however, a definite Taoist strain in all his thinking and writing.

Whether he writes of law or literature, his manuscript is a palimpsest, with the Taoist or Buddhist (these are much the same) reflections showing through.

I do not know of any other outstanding lawyer in any country, who combines in himself such apparent opposites, for we do not associate the legal mind with either poetry or mysticism. Legal rationalism and poetic sensitivity seem to belong to different personalities. Yet, in the author's case, these are blended into a perfect unison. This may explain his penetrative insight into the souls of the T'ang poets.

Even when he writes on law, he is poetic. Take this, for instance, from his *Fountain of Justice, A Study in the Natural Law:*

*The common law is full of fringes and penumbra, full of shades and nuances; this is what makes it so human, so attractive, and so natural. In the enchanted garden of common law, there are many shady groves which cheer the heart and refresh your spirit at the same time that they lure you on to new vistas. It is not a closed garden, but one which is continuous with the wild fields, hills and rivers on one side, and leads to the streets and marketplaces on the other.*

Where else, in treatises on common law, do we read such an interpretation? One might be pardoned for thinking that all this was a description of the "Garden of Golden Valley" that Pan Yun-tuan built outside Shanghai back in the 16th century. But no, it is a description of common law. But, let us read on, for we are still in the garden:

*At first, you feel all but lost in the labyrinthine ways and paths; you want to discover some design, but you find none. But daily saunterings in the garden familiarize you gradually with the genie of the place, the atmosphere, the ever-changing moods of the garden, with the inevitable result that you are more and more fascinated by it.*

This is Taoist poetry. And indeed, one can almost visualize that moon gate, that Pan Yun-tuan erected at the entrance to his garden, over which was the sign "Chien Chia," meaning "Beauty penetrates gradually." This was what the author wrote of common law.

Yet, there is no garden without its gardener. And so we read:

*"You begin to divine a certain vague design. You do not find a general design, except perhaps the design of nature or of a mysterious Providence."*

Here the Christian over-writes the Taoist on the palimpsest.

It is now more than thirty years since I was first impressed with the poetic mind of this lawyer. How I read and reread his "Random Notes on the Shih Ching," published in T'ien Hsia, that outstanding literary journal of the thirties. I was like Keats discovering Chapman. Had it not been for the format and a working knowledge of the Shih Ching, I would hardly have known where the odes ended and the commentary by the author began. It was something between a classical Greek play and a Japanese Noh performance. From the opening lines of the translated Chinese ode to the last word of the commentary, one unbroken musical score.

The peasants of primitive China were singing their songs to the 20th century and a modern could understand them. That was the genius of the author. He knew the singers as they worked in the fields of millet, repaired the river dikes, or gathered marshmallows at the time of the Ch'ing Ming festival, and he sensed the meaning of their songs. For the first time the Shih Ching appeared in English as the saga of pre-Confucian China. One learned from it more than all the tomes of the archaeologists, ethnologists, and historians, could ever teach.

Vibrant with life, his voice clear and meaningful, the singer and his song lived again in the 20th century.

Then came the author's "Lao Tzu." Surely, the very thing for a legal mind, with its abstruse philosophy and brahmanic insight. Many a sinologue, both Eastern and Western, have set themselves to discover what Lao Tzu, or whoever wrote the "Tao Te Ching," really meant. But there have been as many interpreters as translators. And, withal, the secret remained as elusive as before. But John C. H. Wu saw in the "Tao Te Ching" a charming poem, or perhaps I might say, a prose-poem, which had much in common with what the mystics of all times and places had sought to say. For, do they "not only think and feel alike but use almost the same images in their musings?"

It may be a far cry from the author of the "Tao Te Ching" to the writer of "The Anticipation," but John C. H. Wu was convinced that "nine lines of Traherne's poem form a better interpretation or commentary of the fundamental starting points of Lao Tzu than all his rationalistic commentators have ever offered."

So it was that, as in his *Fountain of Justice,* common law became as a garden, so in his treatment of the "Tao Te Ching," the hitherto inexplicable was transmuted into a mystical prose-poem, shot through and through with all the yearnings of the mystical mind.

It is not surprising, then, that our author has approached the T'ang poets in his own characteristic manner.

Certainly the field is large, for there were no less than 2,200 known poets of that dynasty, who between them managed to compose 48,900 poems. No wonder that translators and commentators, through the centuries, have varied in their choices, with their likes and dislikes.

It is doubtful if all the poems known to the T'ang dynasty have survived the ravages of times in spite of the claim that the collection compiled during the Ch'ing dynasty was a complete anthology. During the reign of Emperor Ch'ien Lung (1735–95) an anonymous elector, noting that Confucius had selected 311 songs from the vast storehouse of antiquity, which he considered best suited for the moral improvement of his own age, resolved to do likewise. So, from the thousands of T'ang poems he close some 300 as a "family reader for children," expressing the optimistic opinion that "whoever can read and understand these poems will be able to write his own poems," a competence which at that time was regarded as essential to the formation of a good Confucian character.

However, we must give credit to the "Retired Scholar of the Lotus Pool," as this selector styled himself, for one thing. He improved on Confucius and that is saying something. He did not include in his selection any poem such as the "Pin Chih Ch'u Yen," which Confucius had given a place in the Shih Ching.

This was probably the world's first testament of a reformed alcoholic:

*And when the guests have drunk their fill,*

*What bellowing, what brawling!*
*Dishes they overturn and spill*
*With posturing and sprawling.*
*'Tis so, when thus far they have gone,*
*Unconscious of offending,*
*Caps all awry, and barely on,*
*Their gambols seem unending.*

However, the Duke Wu of Wei saw the error of his ways and decided no more to join the boys in their convivial sprees. He was quite sober when he set down his closing reflection:

*If with three cups the wits be gone*
*What if you venture on and on?*

Possibly Confucius included this as one of his 311 poems in the hope of forming something like Alcoholics Anonymous.

The "Retired Scholar of the Lotus Pool" was not going to offend the taste of the children, for whom his selection was designed, by any such poem.

Other selectors have been guided more by their literary urges. These scholastics, if we may use that term, have been more concerned with literary style and guided by the presence in the poems of perfect or permissible rhymes, the number of lines in a poem and the number of characters in a line, rather than by any moral message of the poet. Of such selectors, especially among Chinese of all centuries since the days of the T'angs, the number is legion, and, indeed, it might be said that they developed a new art, very mechanistic, that at times seemed completely divorced from the study of poetry as such.

The present author has struck deeper than either the moralists or the scholastics. He has succeeded in sensing the presence of gold that has escaped the notice of both the puritan and the pedant. As a result, we have in the following pages a Poetical History of the T'ang Dynasty. And surely no period in the history of China was so rich in gold, with the finest capital city in the world, the world's first university, attended by students from more than twenty different countries, and breathing a spirit of catholicity unknown elsewhere. Paris was but an enlarged village on the banks of the Seine, London but a fort beside a muddy stream, and Berlin not yet dreamed of, when merchants of many lands

wandered up and down the streets of Ch'angan and a Chinese Mae-
cenas, in the person of Emperor Hsuan Tsung, delighted to attract to
that city the noblest and most accomplished minds of the time.

And what a mecca Ch'angan was! Especially for artists, especially
poets. Li Po, Meng Hao-jan, Wang Wei and Ho Chih-chang, to mention just a few. And the historian Ssu Ch'eng-chen, the essayist Lu
Tsang-yung, Chang Yin the painter of landscapes and Wu Tao-tsu,
whom Japan was to adopt as Godoshi and honor as the "revered father
of Japanese painting." All these and many more met under royal
patronage, painting each other's portraits, criticizing each other's
verses, and drinking each other's wine. A prototype of Goethe's circle
at Weimar and the pre-Raphaelite school in England, but larger and
grander than either. And with a more secure guarantee of immortality.

Many a fine picture and many a stimulating discussion and even
many more inspiring poems, some of which we shall read in the following pages, were born in that enlightened company.

Rarely, if ever, were the circumstances more congenial for the advent
of the Muse, in the person of Wen Ch'ang, who, always before a
cultural renaissance, descended from his celestial home in Ursa Major,
the constellation of the Great Bear, to preside over the new flowering of
both letters and the arts. I like the author's reference to this T'ang
blossoming:

*For nearly thirteen centuries after Christ, poetry in Europe, with the insignificant
exception of Juvenal, kept a death-like silence. It hibernated so long that when it
woke up again in the person of Dante, the last poetic voice it could remember was
that of Virgil, who had laid down his harp just before Christ was born. It seems as
though our Mother Earth purposely rocked Europe to sleep for some time that she
might teach Asia to sing. And what difference did it make to God whether his
children were singing in Asia or Europe, so long as He could hear some sweet music
in the course of every twenty-four hours!*

The author has well titled his study of T'ang poetry, for the poets he
deals with reflect, in their poems, the temper of the times, the four
seasons of the T'ang dynasty. This is all so very Chinese. The earliest
songs of the people, from princes to peasants, told of their joys and
sorrows and their attitude towards the ruler. In the days of Chou, it was
the custom of the Emperor, accompanied by his Officer of History and
his Master of Music, to make regular visits to the feudal states for the

express purpose of collecting copies of the ballads and ditties the people were singing, in order to sense their temper. And yet, was it so peculiarly Chinese after all, for did not a Scottish earl once say, "If I could compose the ballads of the people, I would not care who made their laws?"

These four seasons are much more than the phases of a lunar year; they are the register of the psychological mutations of the human spirit. The author has this in mind as he interprets the moods of T'ang and his method is most strongly reminiscent of Shakespeare himself.

> Now is the winter of our discontent
> Made glorious summer by this sun of York,
> And all the clouds that lowered upon our house
> In the deep bosom of the ocean buried.

The poems are the accents of those phases of the human struggle. Not just clever arrangements of a certain number of Chinese characters in a certain number of lines. Not mechanisms but microcosms, in which are bespoken the entire gamut of emotions. Laughter, conviviality, wonder, meditation, and, as in the case of Li Yu, the perils of the dark night of the soul.

Yet were not his songs among the most deeply-charged with emotion of all the T'ang outpourings? The Muse may have drawn a veil over its face in those days of the T'ang dissolution, but still, like the nightingale, which, bereft of its young, fills the woods with the music of woe, and, from the impulse of its sorrow, warbles its sweetest strains, so sang Li Yu of the days that had been, of past springs and summers.

Now it was the time of Götterdämmerung. Everywhere the gods were toppling over. It was night and cold. The Southern T'ang was beginning to dissolve and Li Yu, himself a Prince of T'ang, felt the shivers in his own soul. But he sang on. Our author hears the song and diagnoses the spiritual mood of the singer. "Only a miracle can save the world from another deluge and there are no miracles."

This present study of T'ang poetry is, I believe, the first convincing attempt to penetrate beneath the surface and catch a glimpse of what was really going on inside the minds of the poets as they brushed their characters, some in haste, but mostly at leisure, that is if mental and spiritual alertness can be associated with leisure. Perhaps it were better to say worldly inactivity.

One may say, then, that the Four Seasons of T'ang Poetry are a study of Life, not just as it was in T'ang China but everywhere and at all times. Variants there will be as the sun is warmer in some places and the wintry winds strike deeper into the bones than in other places, but always spring gives birth to the singer of lusty songs, whereas autumn shows the lengthening of the shadows and the strewing of the road of life with autumn leaves.

Always and everywhere a Li Po opens the gate and a Li Yu closes it.

One has not always to agree with the author's interpretation of certain poets and their songs. He himself would be the last to demand this. But one thing is clear. The author has gone beyond the study of the poets' technique and laid bare their souls. This had called for a penetrative acumen, most uncommon among translators of Chinese poetry.

Perhaps, at some other time, the author will carry further a thought he has hinted at in the case of Li Po. He refers to Li's "variety of moods" and his "iconoclastic tendency."

This is a departure from the orthodox interpretation that Li Po was just a boisterous reveller. But does it go far enough? What was this iconoclast attempting to break down and destroy? When he lifted the wine cup to "drown the sorrows of ten thousand ages," was he just making a drunken gesture? Could it have been that his poems, or some of them, were protests in an age that knew nothing of box orators and campaigners marching along city streets, with banners flying, and shouting their slogans? Were those poems designed to flay, often with cutting satire, the growing and destructive luxury of the T'ang court and the deadening effects of the bureaucracy that regimentation was spawning? Remember his poem in praise of Yang Kuei-fei, ordered by Ming Huang, in which he compared the first concubine to the "Flying Swallow" that wrecked the House of Han!

Perhaps—it is just a thought—Li Po despaired of things and the way things were going and took to the cup. A Chinese Omar. Centuries later, the Persian poet, in his quest for truth, visited one pundit after another, only to be baffled more than ever, and withal, to come out "by that same door as in I went." Futility of futilities, all is futility. And so, Omar too became an iconoclast like Li Po, and, amid his cups, dreamed of shattering to bits "this sorry scheme of things entire" and then remoulding it in a shape "nearer to the heart's desire."

After all, most poets are intoxicated. Li Po by the sight of the moon, Shelley by the beauty of Italian hills, Wordsworth by a field of daffo-dils, Shakespeare by the radiance of a starry night, Keats by the song of a nightingale, Tennyson by such a small thing as a crimson petal, and mystics throughout the ages by God.

However, in order that the reader may gain the fullest appreciation of the following pages and the author's unique interpretation of T'ang poetry, a brief outline of the times in which these poems were com-posed might prove a valuable aid.

The T'ang dynasty was founded in A.D. 618 by a young man, Li Shih-min, whose military skill enabled him to eliminate all other contenders for the Dragon Throne, left vacant when Sui Emperor Yang Ti shut himself up in his pleasure palace at Yangchow in the company of many beautiful ladies. With true Confucian filialism, Li Shih-min set his father Li Yuan on the empty throne, but it was no place for him. He preferred the open spaces. The wild blood of his non-Chinese mother, who had come from the region beyond the Great Wall, coursed strongly through his veins. For eight years Li Yuan tried playing the role of Emperor and then gave it up.

Li Shih-min succeeded him as Emperor T'ai Tsung and during the twenty-two years of his reign, set the firm foundations of what was to become China's Golden Age.

He was a great innovator, as most men, in China and elsewhere, who possess independent minds have always been. The bureaucrats tried their hand at pushing him around, but T'ai Tsung was determined to do the pushing. He selected competent men outside the ranks of the graduates, who had gained honor-passes at the public examinations, and appointed these to assist in the government of the country. Poets, though not outstanding in their knowledge of Confucian lore, were regarded as worthy of official rank. Later, he added historians, lawyers, and mathematicians.

From the outset he realized that China needed security. So his armies extended the bounds of empire right into the heart of Asia. It was wise, he concluded, to keep potential enemies at the greatest possible distance.

This accomplished, T'ai Tsung got down to the job that was nearest to his heart, the strengthening and broadening of the national culture. He believed, wise man as he was, that culture was China's greatest asset. Soldiers, politicians, economists and the rest, had their part to play, but it was a minor one. The scholar must be regarded as the most important man in the country. As the culture-bearer, he would carry the torch of civilization into the realms of the uncivilized. The rays of the enlightenment would radiate from Ch'angan, the capital of the T'ang.

And so, in A.D. 630, the third year of Cheng-kuan, he founded the Academy of Ch'angan, which, during his lifetime, became the most accomplished seat of learning in the world. Students from many countries filled its halls, including both Jews and Moslems. As Christianity entered China during his reign, there were probably Christian students also.

Emperor T'ai Tsung was, without doubt, the most enlightened and, in his outlook, the most catholic of all the rulers, who in those years sat on the thrones of the kingdoms of this world. And it is worthy of note that one of the greatest influences, that made him what he was, was his Empress. She was the power behind the throne and it is on record that she made T'ai Tsung promise, when on her death-bed, that instead of lavishing vast sums on building her tomb, he would devote the money to the erection of a library in connection with the Academy. Her sole request was that she should be buried without much ceremony but within sight of the Academy.

T'ang T'ai Tsung himself died in 635 and was succeeded by his son, known to history as Emperor Kao Tsung. For the next thirty-four years he remained on the throne, kept there by the loyalty of his court rather than by any genius or merit on his own part. In fact the only redeeming thing he ever did was to assist the King of Silla in South Korea in bringing the Korean peninsula under one government for the first time. As for the territory his father had brought under Chinese suzerainty in Central Asia, he managed to lose most of it.

A beautiful but ambitious woman was the cause of his downfall; not an infrequent happening in Chinese history. He had made the fatal mistake of recalling from a Buddhist monastery a nun who had been one of his father's concubines. One record has it that his Empress was really responsible for the choice as she was jealous of the attention her husband was paying a certain lady of the palace. Just how the presence of the erstwhile nun was to alleviate that jealousy was not made clear by the annalist.

Be that as it may, when the nun left the nunnery, she took with her to the palace not only her beauty but also her boundless ambition. And such was her skill that, in a short time, she not only got rid of the certain lady but also the Empress herself. Now that the field was clear Wu Tse-t'ien came out from behind the lattices into the open. The time had not yet come to seat herself on the throne but, in the meantime, she could direct things from behind it. She was patient for she knew that her imperial dupe would not live a day longer than she decided.

That day came in the year 684. Emperor Kao Tsung died. Whether from natural cause or human design, it matters little. If the Chinese annalist had any suspicion, he thought it wise to keep such to himself.

Then, for the next six years, there was the usual scramble. So it appeared, but the clever Wu Tse-t'ien was playing her hand. In the year 690 she tired of the puppets and made the plunge that landed her square on the throne, and there she remained for the next fifteen years, ruling China with an iron hand, officiating at the imperial sacrifices, and, in the intervals, getting rid of all who dared to oppose her. Of course, she was not the first woman in Chinese history to do this, but this former nun did create one record, she changed the dynastic name. T'ang became Chou.

Whether the tales of her private life, that swept like foul odors through the court of Ch'angan, were true or not, is of little importance. Whether she did have more than a passing interest in a certain Buddhist priest or not and if the charges of incest in the case of her brother had any basis in fact or were just spiteful court rumors, there were, at least, two counts to her credit. She did restore, to some extent, Chinese prestige throughout the Tarim Basin country, which had been humbled to the desert dust during the reign of Kao Tsung. And, more important still, as far as the following pages are concerned, she insisted that poetry become a compulsory test in the public examinations. The result was that officials became proficient not only in Confucian and Buddhist lore, but also as poets.

This was to have a profound influence on the future course of Chinese culture.

There can be no gold without dross. If there had been much of this latter during the dictatorship of this woman, who, at the age of eighty, was deposed, she had prepared the way for that Golden Age that was about to dawn. As will be noted in the following pages, many of the

T'ang poets were or had been officials, and, to a great extent, credit for this must go to Empress Wu and her innovations.

The year 712 came, radiant with promise. The Golden Age had come. As the reader turns the following pages, he will not fail to see Ch'angan, the brilliant capital of the T'angs on the bank of the River Wei in Shensi Province, and, from it, luminous rays, like pencils of sparkling jade, shooting out in all directions. The coruscation was particularly clear in Japan, from which little-known land in the East students flocked to the Chinese capital and then returned to build their city of Nara on the model of Ch'angan. Rarely, if ever, had so many artists and men of letters been gathered together in one city, and it has been estimated that at one time during the reign of Emperor Hsuan Tsung, generally known as Ming Huang, no less than 20,000 of these were living in the capital, thanks to imperial largesse.

Ch'angan was the symbol of opulence, both material and intellectual. There was nothing like it elsewhere under the sun. It was the epitome of the highest in civilization. While ceaseless trains of camels brought into the city the richest goods of Central Asia and from the lands beyond, and merchants of many lands presided over their marts, with Confucians, Buddhists, Moslems, and Christians mingling together in the streets, and so many Jews that a commissioner had to be appointed to handle Jewish affairs, every art known to man flourished as never before. For the first time in Chinese history a drama school, known as the "Pear Garden," flourished within the precincts of the palace, maintained from the privy purse.

But such splendor could not last. Man is so made that he cannot endure excellence in any form overlong. Sooner or later, the Golden Age becomes insufferable. Beauty is made to be destroyed. Such is the way with our human species, always and everywhere. The pitcher must, sooner or later, be broken at the fountain of clear running water.

So it was with the Golden Age of the T'ang.

One by one, the sections of the empire beyond the Great Wall began to break away. Corruption in high places, typified by the infamous Li Lin-fu, gradually rotted away the very foundations of the State. Then, as though to complete the destruction, beauty mingled with guile entered the door of the palace. "Many men can build a State but it takes only one woman to destroy it." A Chinese proverb, but a universal truism.

Summer had come and gone. It was now autumn and the chilly winds of winter, with their "ice-piercing crystals," were already beginning to blow over Ch'angan from the northeast.

Yang Kuei-fei, a former concubine of a T'ang prince, won the attention of Emperor Hsuan Tsung, who took her into his palace. And with her went her sisters, the "Flowers of Yang," and her brother. From that time, the atmosphere in the palace and indeed throughout the court became poisoned. Slowly but surely the entire tissue system of the Golden Age began to feel the baneful effect as the poison spread through the T'ang organism, presaging death.

It is not clear whether Yang Kuei-fei was in league with An Lu-shan, the commander of the garrison of Yen, the site of later Peking, or not. But it is a fact of history that in the year 755 he unfurled the standard of revolt and marched on the capital. The Emperor fled, taking Yang Kuei-fei with him. On their southwest route, the guard of the imperial bodyguard, convinced that the concubine was the cause of the disaster, demanded her death. Helpless to resist, the Emperor had to hand her over. And on a pear tree in an orchard, she was hanged. The story is fully told in Po Chü-i's famous ballad in later pages of this volume.

It is recorded that that rebellion, led by An Lu-shan, cost China not less than twelve million lives.

But even that was not the most grievous loss to China for the civil war marked the beginning of the end of the T'ang dynasty. It is true that the descendants of the House of Li held the throne for another one hundred years, but none ever succeeded in restoring the glory that had been. Had it not been for the rising power of the eunuchs, something of that splendor might have been regained, for at times there were signs, bright with hope, but these proved to be but the hectic glows of an expiring splendor, coronals of an evanescent brightness on hills, distant and ever receding.

In the year 907 the night set in and everywhere there was darkness.

In the gloom, without one single star to light the way, one last ray of hope to inspire, the remnant of the T'angs fled south. There, like the Jews during their Babylonian captivity fifteen centuries earlier, they had to "hang their harps upon the willow trees" for the soul of T'ang poetry was in exile. Crossing the Yangtze, they sought refuge among the hills of Kwangsi, the plains of Kwangtung, and the upper reaches of the River Min in Fukien. A few were to go further till they halted on what is known now as the Kowloon Peninsula.

But they produced no songbirds.

Sufficient for them and their descendants to call themselves, with pride, "Men of T'ang."

All these fluctuations in the history of the T'ang dynasty may be of some help to the reader as he turns the pages of *Four Seasons of T'ang Poetry*.

# INTRODUCTION:
# THE GOLDEN AGE

IT HAS BEEN CUSTOMARY to divide the poetry of T'ang into four periods: Early T'ang, Golden T'ang, Middle T'ang, and Late T'ang. The first period was just a kind of overture; the second included Wang Wei, Li Po, and Tu Fu; the third included Po Chü-i, Yuan Chen, Han Yu and his circle; the fourth included Li Shang-yin, Tu Mu, and Wen T'ing-yuen. This classification was made avowedly without reference to social and political changes, but solely with reference to the art of poetry itself. For instance, a great part of the Golden Period of poetry was anything but golden from the standpoint of political stability and social welfare.

Some of our contemporary historians of Chinese literature have divided the poetry of T'ang into just two periods: the period of Li Po, and the period of Tu Fu. Li Po is said to sum up all the previous poets of T'ang, and Tu Fu is said to open up a new era for all its later poets. This classification has the charm of simplicity. And also it has the merit of not entirely ignoring the environmental changes. There can be no doubt that Li and Tu, who were born within twelve years of each other, do belong to different periods in point of poetry as well as in point of life. I think it is within limits to say that Li Po had written his best poems before the rebellion of An Lu-shan, while the masterpieces of Tu Fu were mostly produced after that event. It has always seemed to me that Li Po sang best when he was happy, while Tu Fu sang best when he was angry. Li Po was a lark singing at heaven's gate; Tu Fu was a nightingale, singing with his throat against a thorn. The glorious early reign of Ming Huang furnished the proper environment for the blithe Li Po; just as the tragic end of the same great Emperor provided the stage for the passionate singing of Tu Fu. It is true that they both belong to the reign of Ming Huang, but then we must remember that Ming Huang himself was torn between two different periods.

I therefore think that the new classification shows a more profound historical insight than the older one. But then it suffers from over-simplification. It ignores real differences between, let us say, the poetry of Li Shang-yin and that of Han Yu, to mention just a few instances. Recently, browsing over a considerable portion of the poems of the whole T'ang period, I have arrived at a classification which seems to me more natural and true to fact than either of the two I have mentioned. I feel that the poetry of T'ang falls naturally into four seasons: Spring, Summer, Autumn and Winter.

The Spring period includes the earliest T'ang bards and Wang Wei and Li Po. The Summer period includes Tu Fu and some poets who wrote about war. The Autumn period includes Po Chü-i and his circle, and Han Yu and his circle. Winter period includes Li Shang-yin, Tu Mu, Wen T'ing-yuen, Hsu Hun, Lo Yin, Han Wu, and many other minor poets.

Seasons are, of course, interpenetrated, one with the other, but on the whole they are distinct enough. I shall not try to define them, but I hope the reader will gradually see and feel what I have in mind as we proceed patiently together in our journey throughout the whole year.

But in order not to keep my readers too much on the guess, I will pick up a spring poet to describe Spring, a summer poet to describe Summer, an autumn poet to describe Autumn, and a winter poet to describe Winter. Here is what Li Po says of Spring:

*The heart of Spring is heaving like waves.*
*The sorrows of Spring are flying about in confusion like snowflakes.*
*All emotions are roused, forming a mingled yarn of joy and grief.*
*O, what pathos I feel within me in this sweetest of the seasons!*

Next let us hear how Tu Fu sighs on a Summer night:

*What a long day it has been! It looked as though the sun would never set!*
*The boiling heat has almost smoked and steamed me to death.*

*Ah for a wind of ten thousand li in length*
*To come wandering from the sky and blow upon my garments like a large fan!*

*Now the bright moon has arisen on the cloudless sky;*
*The leafy trees are sifting its beams like a sieve.*

*In the heart of Summer, the night is all too short.*
*Let me open the pavilion doors to invite the cool air.*

*In the transparent moonlight, every little thing is visible.*
*I can see the winged insects flying and having a good time.*

*One touch of nature makes all creatures kin:*
*Big or small, they all love freedom and comfort.*

*I am only thinking of the soldiers, who, heavy laden with arms,*
*Stand guard at the frontiers for years on end.*

*They have no way of bathing themselves in fresh waters;*
*In the grip of heat, they look despairingly at one another.*

*Throughout the night, the long-handled pans keep the noisy watches;*
*Throughout an endless stretch of land, no soothing silence is to be found.*

*Even if they wear honors thick on their heads,*
*The happiness is nothing like an early return home.*

*Hark! the melancholy notes of flageolets are coming from the northern city.*
*Above my head, the cranes are wheeling about and calling.*

*My gizzard is fretted once more.*
*When, O when will peace and prosperity come back again?*

Now we shall calm down a bit and lend our ears to Po Chü-i philosophizing about Autumn:

## THOUGHTS IN AUTUMN

*The moon has arisen and shines upon the northern hall;*
*The steps and the courtyard are drenched in its clear light.*
*A cool breeze is blowing from the west;*
*The grass and trees are withering day and night.*
*The wu-t'ung and the willows have begun to shed their green leaves.*
*The lovely colors of the orchids are fading.*
*Affected by these things, I meditate privately,*
*And find my heart in a similar condition.*
*Who can always retain his childhood and youth?*
*There is a time for blooming, and a time for decaying.*
*Human life is like a spark from the stone.*
*We often start too late to enjoy ourselves.*

The following lines are taken from Li Shang-yin's poems on Winter:

> *The sun rose in the east,*
> *The sun has set in the west.*
> *The lady Phoenix flies alone,*
> *The female Dragon has become a widow.*
>
>       \*      \*      \*
>
> *Frozen walls and hoary-headed frosts*
> *Join in weaving gloom and sending doom*
> *To the flowers, whose tender roots are snapped asunder,*
> *And whose fragrant souls have breathed their last!*
>
>       \*      \*      \*
>
> *The wax candles weep tears of blood,*
> *Lamenting the coming of the dawn.*

Of course, I don't mean that in the Spring period of T'ang poetry poets were singing only of Spring; in the Summer period, only of Summer; and in Autumn and Winter, only of Autumn and Winter. In fact, the same season or the same scene may evoke quite different feelings in poets of different types. For instance:

> *Night's candles are burnt out, and jocund day*
> *Stands tiptoe on the misty mountain tops.*

Do you not feel that it is a springy voice that you are hearing? But compare these lines of the great Spring bird Shakespeare with Li Shang-yin's:

> *The wax candles weep tears of blood,*
> *Lamenting the coming of the dawn.*

Both may be equally beautiful; but the former represents the beauty of hope, and the latter—the beauty of despair. Read these lines by Li Po:

> *Natural and unadorned, the lotus flowers*
> *Are swinging freely on translucent water.*

This is what I would call Spring in Summer. But read this from Li Shang-yin:

> *The banana tree refuses to unfold its leaves;*
> *The clove remains a closed bud for ever.*
> *Each nurses a private sorrow in its bosom,*
> *Though all breathe the same Spring air.*

This is what I call Winter in Spring.

To take an instance which may be more familiar to my English readers, Wordsworth has always appeared to me to be the Po Chü-i of England. He represents Autumn at its best. He is so ripe and mellow and pensively calm. Even the leaping of his heart when he sees a rainbow has not much of the Spring in it, because his heart leaps within the bounds of "natural piety." In fact, no one knows himself so well as Wordsworth does. The other day, I came across one of his poems which confirms my hunch about him so breathtakingly that I really cannot resist the temptation of quoting it even at the risk of appearing irrelevant to my present theme:

### THE NIGHTINGALE AND THE STOCK DOVE

> O Nightingale! thou surely art
> A creature of a "fiery heart":—
> These notes of thine—they pierce and pierce;
> Tumultuous harmony and fierce!
> Thou singest as if the God of wine
> Has helped thee to a valentine;
> A song in mockery and despite
> Of shades, and dews, and silent night;
> And steady bliss, and all the loves
> Now sleeping in these peaceful groves.
> I heard a Stock dove sing or say
> His homely tale, this very day;
> His voice was buried among trees,
> Yet to be come at by the breeze:
> He did not cease; but cooed—and cooed;
> And somewhat pensively he wooed:
> He sang of love with quiet blending,
> Slow to begin and never ending;
> Of serious faith and inward glee;
> That was the song—the song for me!

This quotation is not so irrelevant to my purpose as it may appear. For if the reader will keep it in mind that the Nightingale, a creature of a "fiery heart," is none other than Tu Fu, and the Stock dove, who signs or says his homely tale, is none other than Po Chü-i, he has already done more than half in understanding T'ang poetry. And if, in addition, he will take to heart these lines of Wordsworth, this time addressed to

a Skylark, he will have acquired a valuable clue to the songs of the
early T'ang poets, especially Li Po:

> *There is madness about thee, and joy divine*
> *In that song of thine.*
>
>             \*         \*         \*
>
>    *Joyous as morning*
> *Thou art laughing and scorning.*
>
>             \*         \*         \*
>
> *Alas! my journey, rugged and uneven,*
> *Through prickly moors or dusty ways must wind;*
> *But hearing thee, or others of thy kind,*
> *As full of gladness and free of heaven,*
> *I, with my fate contented, will plod on,*
> *And hope for higher raptures, when life's day is done.*

With the spring poets, there is something blithe and sprightly about
their joys and sorrows, and their wishes and dreams. One feels that even
their tears sparkle and shine. How do you like this little poem by a
contemporary of Li Po about a girl's dream:

> *O drive away the orioles!*
> *Don't let them sing on the branches!*
> *Their noisy songs have interrupted my dream*
> *Before I could reach the land of my heart's desire!*

How flighty are the fancies and dreams of Li Po:

> *The south wind blows my heart homeward.*
> *See how it flies and lights just before the old wine-shop!*

What a different world you are in when you read Li Shang-yin's:

> *O my heart, blow not with the Spring flowers!*
> *My love-thoughts are turned to ashes as soon as they sprout.*

Naturally, Spring is not without its sorrows, even to a spring poet. Li
Po, for instance, wrote:

> *I hear the sweet notes of the water-nut song,*
> *Making me tumble under the load of Spring.*

But it is one thing to "tumble under the load of Spring." It is quite
another thing to feel, as Li Shang-yin does:

*My heart is broken even before Spring comes.*

The wishes and even dreams of a summer poet are like thunder; when, for instance, Tu Fu felt pent up on a hot autumn day, he thundered:

> *With a heavy girdle around my waist, I am maddened by the heat,*
> *   I feel like uttering a loud cry!*
> *And my subordinates are still pestering me with piles upon piles of*
> *   documents!*
> *On the southern side I see such green pines hanging over a little pool,*
> *Ah for layers upon layers of ice on which to walk barefooted!*

How differently an autumn poet would feel in hot Summer. Po Chü-i's poem on "How to keep cool in Summer" contains these philosophic lines:

> *How to clear off the vexing heat?*
> *By sitting quietly in your house.*
> *   \*        \*        \**
> *A calm heart can scatter the heat;*
> *An empty room induces coolness to come.*

I don't know exactly how Li Po feels when the weather is very hot, but I am pretty sure that his soul would fly up to the snowcapped mountains until he forgets his poor body which he has left behind him in a seething cauldron.

Of course, even a winter poet is not impervious to heat. But I should think his soul would not fly up to the snow-capped mountains, nor would he possess enough spiritual vigor to drive away the heat, or enough physical energy to utter a loud shriek. At most he would emit a whimpering wish that some of these days cooler weather may come, or that some mythical goblin, in which he half believes, would work a miracle for him. This is exactly the sentiment I find in a beautiful poem by one of Li Shang-yin's younger contemporaries, Wang Ku:

### A BALLAD OF BOILING HEAT

> *The god of fire hails from the south,*
> *Whipping the fiery dragon on which he rides.*
> *Flags of fire are fluttering all over the air,*
> *Until the skies are burned red hot.*
> *The wheel of the sun hangs over our heads,*
> *Motionless, as if nailed to the skies.*

> *All the nations of the world boil*
> *As in a seething cauldron!*
> *The lovely green of the Five Mountains is scorched,*
> *And the beautiful colors of the clouds vanish.*
> *Even the Ocean has become a frying pan;*
> *Its waves of sorrow are dried up.*
> *I wish only that one of these evenings*
> *A silvery breeze will rise,*
> *To sweep away for me*
> *The heat of the whole world!*

By this time, you may be wondering how a winter poet would feel in Winter. Well, I have just found a poem by Liu Chia, another late T'ang poet, called "A Song of Bitter Cold":

> *All streams are frozen, swallowing their sobs.*
> *My songs are more and more steeped in sadness.*
> *In the midnight I still stand leaning against a pine tree,*
> *Until my clothes are full of snow.*

> *The sugar-cane has its sweet end and its bitter end:*
> *I only like to cleave to the bitter end!*
> *Some birds sing songs of joy, others songs of grief:*
> *I only love that bird which sings with blood flowing from his beak!*

This is what I would call winter dourness, despair turned into desperation. What a contrast it offers to the feeling of that summer bird Tu Fu in a similar weather:

> *Ah for a big mansion of a thousand, or ten thousand rooms*
> *To give shelter and cheer to all the poor scholars of the world!*
> *Safe from the ravages of wind and rain, they will feel as calm as the*
>     *mountain.*
> *Ah me! The day on which I shall see such a mansion rise before my eyes,*
> *I shall be happy to continue to live in this broken hut and frozen to*
>     *death all alone.*

Indeed, Tu Fu is the most Christ-like poet that I know!

The Spring of T'ang poetry is Dionysian; the Summer is Promethean; the Autumn is Epimethean; and the Winter—O, what shall I call it? I have no name for it. But whenever I read the winter poets, I am reminded of that indescribably fascinating poem of Christina Rossetti's "Passing Away" and I often catch myself humming this stanza from "The Bride-Song" in her poem, "The Prince's Progress":

> Ten years ago, five years ago,
>     One year ago,—
> Even then you had arrived in time,
>     Though somewhat slow;
> Then you had known her living face,
>     Which now you cannot know;
> The frozen fountain would have leaped,
>     The buds gone on to blow,
> The warm south wind would have awaked
>     To melt the snow.

Just now, after re-reading this stanza, I find myself reciting a poem by Tu Mu, another winter poet:

### SIGHING OVER A FLOWER

> O! How I hate myself for coming so late
>     In search of the flower!
> Years ago, I saw her before she had blown—
>     Just a budlet was she!
> Now I find the wind has made a havoc of her—
>     Her petals strew the ground!
> I only see a tree thick with leaves—
>     And branches full of fruits!

And what wintry despair one finds in this poem by Hsü Hun, another contemporary of Li Shang-yin:

### THE DYING WORDS OF A FRIEND

> From a family of scholars I have come;
>     I have only a few children.
> In my life, my friends have been kind to me,
>     But I have not repaid their kindness.
> This morning, I shall be buried far from home—
>     At the foot of a chilly hill!
> Tell, O tell my tender-hearted old mother
>     Not to wait any more at the doorsill!

How these poems remind me of T. S. Eliot's lines:

*This is the way the world ends*
*This is the way the world ends*
*This is the way the world ends*
*Not with a bang but a whimper.*

I don't regard Eliot as a winter poet, but certainly he describes the wintry spirit very well. I don't know about the world, but I certainly know this is the way the poetry of T'ang ends, "not with a bang but a whimper." A whimper, yes. But what a whimper!

The poetry of the last of the T'angs is like a tubercular girl of surpassing beauty. You may admire her secretly, and at a distance. But to fall in love with her would be fatal. And yet, at times, you are so entranced by her beauty that you feel the question of life and death becomes quite a paltry matter.

Ever since the close of T'ang, China has been whimpering for more than ten centuries. Not until now does she feel some stirrings in her soul which look very much like the beginning of a new Spring! When Winter has tarried with us so long, "can Spring be far behind?"

But if there is another Golden Age in store for my country, as I am honestly sure that there is, then let it be even more glorious than T'ang! For the flowering of Chinese culture in T'ang reminds me all too much of a stanza in Richard Le Gallienne's "A Ballad of London":

*Upon thy petals butterflies,*
*But at thy root, some say, there lies*
*A world of weeping trodden things,*
*Poor worms that have not eyes nor wings.*

In the coming age, let Life become Poetry, or else it wouldn't be worthwhile to sing! But lest I should be carried away by my enthusiasm for the future and forget what I am writing about, I'll draw rein and return to my present theme.

On the whole, we may say that in the Spring of T'ang poetry, there were tears without griefs; in its Summer, the poets were so angry at the phenomena of social injustice and the uncalled-for miseries of their fellow-beings that they had very little time to weep for themselves; in its Autumn, griefs were assuaged by copious tears; and in its Winter, there were griefs without tears. And the great wonder of T'ang poetry as a whole is that it was such a complete year in itself, a year in which the seasons seem to come in succession so naturally and inevitably. Like

# SPRING

JOHN STUART MILL once looked around him and sighed that there were
so few eccentrics. It is probably because he lived in the Victorian Age,
which has always appeared to me as the mellow season of Autumn,
when the sense of wonder was a bit worn out and everything tended to
crystallize down into definite forms. It's only in Springtime, when the
very air is full of promise, when people are young in spirit and fresh in
curiosity, when they are stirred by the growing pangs of adolescence,
that the earth will be found teeming with eccentrics. Such a period I
find in the early part of the T'ang Dynasty, that is, from its founding in
A.D. 618 up to somewhere around 735, when the star of Yang Kwei-fei
was beginning to rise and the star of T'ang was beginning to sink.

Right at the opening of the dynasty we come across a most eccentric
Buddhist monk by the name of Wang Fan-chih. His rugged language
and shocking fancies present a marked contrast to the squeamish and
refined banalities of the preceding age. Take this for instance:

> *Fan-chih wears his socks slipshod,*
> *And everybody says it's very odd.*
> *I would rather have your eyes cut out*
> *Than have my feet covered up!*

This is certainly slipshod writing, but at least here is a man who dares to
be himself. What brutal frankness is revealed in this:

> *When I saw that chap die,*
> *My stomach was hot like fire.*
> *Did you think that I cared for that chap?*
> *No, I only feared the same would happen to me!*

And then what ghostly fancies this monk has:

> *None in the world live up to a hundred,*
> *But everybody seems to tune himself up for a thousand*
>  *years.*
> *When you beat iron into doorsills,*
> *The ghosts clap their hands and laugh at you!*

There is another poem which describes his self-sufficiency and has some Whitman-like tang about it:

> *I have opened up a field of ten mow*
> *On the slope of the southern hill.*
> *I have planted a couple of pine trees*
> *And a few rows of green beans.*
> *When it's hot, I take a bath in the lake.*
> *When it's cool, I sing on the shore.*
> *A free lance, I am sufficient as I am.*
> *Who can do anything to me?*

When you hear people sing like this, you feel that the world is beginning once more. The significance of this monk lies in his freedom from the shackles of convention in life as well as in letters. He shattered the mincing art of his immediate predecessors. There is a strange beauty in his wild notes, just as when your eyes, accustomed to see the bound feet of old-fashioned Chinese ladies, suddenly see a country girl with a pair of natural feet about as big as your own.

The next eccentric to attract our attention is the grandfather of Tu Fu, Tu Shen-yen, who was born around 646 and died in his sixties. He seems to have suffered from what modern psychologists would call a delusion of grandeur. He once said, "In the art of letters, Chu Yuan and Sung Yu should serve as my gatekeepers; in the art of calligraphy, Wang Hsi-chih ought to kowtow to me."

I have no means of judging his calligraphy, as he has not left any traces of this particular art. As to his art of letters, I have searched with a miscroscope all his forty-three poems that have come down to us, but have only found four lines of real poetry:

*The Dawn has come out of the ocean attired in robes of rosy gauze.*
*The Spring has waded over the River and arrived among the plums and*
  *willows.*
*The life-giving breath of the season has gilded the feathers of birds*
  *with gold.*
*The clear daylight has dyed the duckweeds in lovely green*

Certainly there is Spring in these lines, and while they hardly justify his self-estimate, they will continue to be recited as long as Chinese poetry will continue to be studied. This reminds me of another poet of the same period, Wang Po, who will live forever in these two lines:

*The existence of a single bosom friend on earth*
*Turns the wide, wide world into a cordial neighborhood.*

We find another interesting character in the person of Ch'en Tzu-ang who was born in 656 and died in his early forties. A native of Szechuen, and a rich man's son, he started his studies late. Only in his late twenties did he go to the capital to take his first degree. As he was still an obscure scholar, he tried to draw public attention to himself by staging a rather spectacular scene. Somebody was selling a Tartar guitar and asked the exorbitant price of a million cash! Tzu-ang bought it at that price, which naturally shocked the spectators. Upon being asked why he did such a foolish thing, he said, "I am an expert player of this kind of guitar." "May we have the pleasure of hearing you play it?" they urged. "O yes," he answered, "I'll give a performance tomorrow in the Hsuan Yang Terrace." The next day, Tzu-ang prepared a grand feast for all. As was to be expected, many people came flocking in to hear his music. But instead of playing the guitar, he made an oration! "Gentlemen," he said, "I am a native of Szechuen, and Ch'en Tzu-ang is my name. I have brought with me a hundred scrolls of my essays and poems, which deserve to be better known. As to this guitar, there is nothing precious about it!" Thereupon he dashed the guitar into pieces, and handed round copies of his writings. In one day, he became the talk of the town! Among the poems distributed were the famous thirty-eight Lyrics. They were written in the old style, but the language was very simple and the thought filled with genuine Taoistic insights and cosmic yearnings. One specimen will suffice:

## BUSINESS MEN

*Business men set store by their cunning skill,*
*But in Wisdom they are puerile still.*
*Outwitting one another in the art of exploitation,*
*They know nothing of man's true destination.*
*Why not emulate the Master of Dark Truth who, 'tis said,*
*Could see the whole universe in a vase of jade?*
*Leaving the world behind, without fetter or bond,*
*On the chariot of Cosmic Process he entered the Beyond!*

Another poem, which many critics have rightly regarded as his master-piece, shows still better the nameless pathos of this newcomer in early Spring:

## GAZING INTO DISTANCE

*I look before, and don't see the ancient sages:*
*I look after, and don't see the coming ages.*
*Only the heaven-and-earth will last through the endless years:*
*Overcome by pathos, my eyes are filled with silent tears.*

The simplicity of his language was a deliberate revolt against rhetoric. In a letter to a friend, Tzu-ang said:

*The art of letters has been decaying for five hundred years. . . . In my leisure hours, I have looked into the poems of the Ch'i and Liang Dynasties, and I could not help sighing when I found all genuine feeling and insight were smothered by meaningless figures of speech and squeamish refinement of words. So much rhetoric and so little sentiment! When will the grand tradition of Shih Ching revive?*

This desire to break with the immediate past and to return to a remoter antiquity is characteristic of all the literary reforms of old China. And this is true of the reforms in other fields as well.

While it may be that Tzu-ang himself has not given us any really first-rate poems, his contribution as a pioneer in the revolt against rhetoric cannot be over-estimated, for he set the pace for the later poets. As Han Yu so justly said:

*The art of letters has prospered in our Dynasty:*
*Tzu-ang it was who first departed from the beaten track.*

In the meantime, Spring is warming up, and more and more birds

come to sing. The 7th century was not to close without having
produced a formidable host of poets. To begin with, there was the
famous Ho Chih-chang who was born in 659 and lived to 744, and who
called himself "a Mad Guest from the Mountain of Sze-ming" (in the
neighbourhood of Ningpo). Exactly how "mad" he was we don't
know, but certainly he had a great liking for wine. Tu Fu wrote a little
caricature of him:

> Chih-chang on horseback swayed back and forth
> As though he were sitting in a boat.
> Dizzy with wine, he fell into the water,
> And was found sleeping on the bottom of a well!

He did not write many poems, but one poem of his, I think, has been
recited more times throughout all these generations than any other
poem in the Chinese language:

### ON RETURNING HOME

> As a young man I left home,
> As an old man I have come back.
> My native accent I still retain,
> But hairs on my head I lack!
> When my boys saw me,
> They didn't know their pa had come home.
> Gingerly they smiled and asked:
> "From where O honorable guest, have you come?"

Among the younger contemporaries of Chih-chang were Liu Shen-
hsu, Chang Chiu-ling, Chang Jo-hsu, Wang Ch'ang-ling, and Wang
Tzu-huan, to mention but a few. Each was the author of quite a few
songs which still continue to live on the lips of many of our contemporaries. I shall only reproduce here representative pieces from each.

### A QUIET STUDY ON A HILL
#### By Liu Shen-Hsu

> The pathways penetrate far into the white clouds.
> The Spring is as long as the green streamlets.
> From time to time, fallen flowers are wafted on the flowing waters,
> Sending puffs of fresh perfume from afar.
> An idle door, facing a mountain path, remains ajar.

*A quiet study is hidden in the midst of thickset willows.*
*The whole place is drenched in empyrean light.*
*Even my clothes acquire a new luster from the clear rays of the sun.*

## SINCE MY LORD LEFT
### By Chang Chiu-ling

*Since my lord left,*
*I have had no heart to spin and weave.*
*Thinking of thee has made me thinner and thinner,*
*Just as the full moon has waned from night to night.*

## A WIFE'S SIGH IN SPRING
### By Wang Ch'ang-ling

*A young woman, newly married, she is a stranger to sorrow.*
*In Spring, dressed in gay array, she climbs up a lovely tower.*
*Suddenly, the green color of the willows meets her eyes.*
*"Ah," she sighs to herself, "why did I let him go to seek glory?"*

## CLIMBING A TOWER
### By Wang Tsu-huan

*The white sun has sunk behind the hills.*
*The Yellow River is pouring into the sea.*
*To see still farther into the horizon,*
*Let us go up one more storey!*

## THE RIVER BY NIGHT IN SPRING
### By Chang Jo-hsu
### Translated by Charles Budd

*In Spring the flooded river meets the tide*
*Which from the ocean surges to the land;*
*The moon across the rolling water shines*
*From wave to wave to reach the distant strand.*

*And when the heaving sea and river meet,*
*The latter turns and floods the fragrant fields;*
*While in the moon's pale light as shimmering sleet*
*Alike seem sandy shores and wooded wealds.*

*For sky and river in one colour blend,*
*Without a spot of dust to mar the scene;*

*While in the heavens above the full-orbed moon*
*In white and lustrous beauty hangs serene.*

*And men and women, as the fleeting years,*
*Are born into this world and pass away;*
*And still the river flows, the moon shines fair,*
*And will their courses surely run for aye.*

*But who was he who first stood here and gazed*
*Upon the river and the heavenly light?*
*And when did moon and river first behold*
*The solitary watcher in the night?*

*The maples sigh upon the river's bank,*
*A white cloud drifts across the azure dome;*
*In yonder boat some traveller sails tonight*
*Beneath the moon which links his thoughts with home.*

*Above the home it seems to hover long,*
*And peep through chinks within her chamber blind;*
*The moon-borne message she cannot escape,*
*Alas, the husband tarries far behind!*

*She looks across the gulf but hears no voice,*
*Until her heart with longing leaps apace,*
*And fain would she the silvery moonbeams follow*
*Until they shine upon her loved one's face.*

*"Last night," she murmured sadly to herself,*
*"I dreamt of falling flowers by shady ponds;*
*My Spring, ah me! half through its course has sped,*
*But you return not to your wedded bonds."*

*Forever onward flows the mighty stream;*
*The Spring, half gone, is gliding to its rest;*
*While on the river and the silent pools*
*The moonbeams fall obliquely from the west.*

*And now the moon descending to the verge*
*Has disappeared beneath the sea-borne dew;*
*While stretch the waters of the "Siao and Siang,"*
*And rocks and cliffs, in never-ending view*

*How many wanderers by tonight's pale moon*
*Have met with those from whom so long apart:—*
*As on the shore midst flowerless trees I stand*
*Thoughts old and new surge through my throbbing heart!*

Now we come to Meng Hao-jan (689–740). By nature a hermit, he once had an interview with Ming Huang. Asked by His Majesty to recite some of his poems, he picked up, for some reason or other, a particular poem which contains these lines:

> Don't present any memorials to the Imperial Court!
> Let me return to my old home among the hills!
> Untalented, I am overlooked by the enlightened Monarch;
> Often ill, I have lost contact with my old friends.

Ming Huang, naturally, was not much pleased by these lines. "Look here," he said, "you are not being fair to me. I have not overlooked you, but you never wanted any office from me. I wish you had recited that poem on T'ung T'ing Lake which contains two lines I like so much:

> Its exhalation warms up the marshy villages;
> Its waves rock the city as in a cradle."

Ming Huang was probably in a sulky mood (it was before he had known Yang Awei-fei), but he was subtle too. For the same poem also has this line in it:

> Living like a hermit, I feel unworthy of the sage Emperor.

Be that as it may, the two gentlemen never saw eash other again.
Li Po had the highest admiration for Hao-jan. He wrote:

> I love my Master Meng!
> Who has not heard of the romance of his life?
> In ruddy youth he renounced worldly honors;
> In gray hairs he nestles amidst clouds and pines.
> Inebriate with the moon, he often hits the peak of bliss.
> Bewitched by the flowers, he refuses to serve the king.
> O high mountain! How can I aspire to you?
> I only look from afar, inhaling your pure fragrance.

I have never seen Li Po praise a man so highly as he does Meng. Perhaps, Meng was even greater as a man than as a poet. But what charming poems on Nature he has left behind him! From his poems one seems to see a man who kept the noiseless tenor of his way "along the cool sequestered vale of life." Let me give some specimens here:

## AN INVITATION TO A FRIEND

*I am enjoying myself here*
*Among the cloud-capped hills.*
*Thinking of you, I have climbed up to the top and gaze afar.*
*My soul flies with the birds until they vanish from my ken.*
*I feel a little sad because it's so near evening;*
*But my spirit is stirring within me in the presence of such a fine sight!*
*From here I can see some people returning to their villages:*
*They walk on the sandy beaches, and tarry around the ferry.*
*The trees that skirt the horizon look like mushrooms;*
*The boats on the river look no bigger than the moon.*
*Why don't you come, bringing some wine along!*
*We shall have a good time together on the Double Nine.*

These lines were written in Autumn, but there is nothing autumnal about them. He is intoxicated with Nature, and naturally he wishes to share his joy with his friends. How he misses his friends is shown in another beautiful poem, of which I beg to use Giles' version:

## IN DREAMLAND

*The Sun has set behind the western slope,*
*    The eastern moon lies mirrored in the pool;*
*With streaming hair my balcony I ope,*
*    And stretch my limbs to enjoy the cool.*
*Loaded with lotus-scent the breeze sweeps by,*
*    Clear dripping drops from tall bamboos I hear,*
*I gaze upon my idle lute and sigh:*
*    Alas no sympathetic soul is near!*
*And so I doze, the while before mine eyes*
*    Dear friends of other days in dream-clad forms arise.*

The most popularly known of all his poems is a little quatrain on "Morning in Spring":

*In Spring how sweet is sleep! I don't know the day has dawned!*
*But what a riotous chorus of birds I hear all around!*
*Last night the sound of wind and rain stole into my ears—*
*I wonder how many flowers have fallen on the ground.*

Perhaps the greatest Nature poet of T'ang was Wang Wei (699–759). With him the Spring of T'ang poetry is at its sweetest. His naturalism

is of the purest brand, unalloyed with any sense of personal disappoint-
ment, as is sometimes the case even with Meng Hao-jan; and undiluted
with pale meditation and sophisticated ratiocination, as is so often the
case with Po Chü-i. Wang Wei is just between the uncomfortable and
awkward stirrings of early Spring and the yeasty madness of late
Spring. His voice is warm and soothing like the fairest days in Spring.
With fancy clear and soul clean, he "takes in all beauty with an easy
span."

His personality is not easy to describe. He is not an eccentric, nor a
fanatic, nor an embittered soul, and yet he is not what my friend Mr.
Wen Yuan-tung would call "a moral smug." He is neither a libertine
nor a prig, neither a wild ass nor a mule either. He does not belong to
that class of dreary souls, who, in the words of Dante, "lived without
blame, and without praise," and "who were neither rebellious nor
faithful to God."

Wang Wei's soul is of the sky-blue tint, and his affinities, to borrow
some words from William James in his description of healthy-minded-
ness, "are rather with flowers and birds and all the enchanting inno-
cencies than with the dark human passions." This man has always impressed me as a man who possesses religious gladness from the very
outset, and needs no deliverance from any antecedent burden. His religion is one of union with the divine, and he sees God not as a severe
Father, but as a tender Mother.

His life was uneventful, and need not be told here at length. Officially,
he was pretty high up. Official life, however, did not vulgarize him in
the least. He was a devoted Buddhist. But the wonder of it was that he
seldom talked of Buddhism in his poems, as Po Chü-i so often did
successively of his Confucianism, his Taoism, and his Buddhism. It is
only when your faith is feeble that you feel the need to buttress it with
arguments; and the irony is that the more arguments you use, the more
is your faith made sickly with the pale cast of thought. You cry your
religion at the top of your voice, as a peddler cries his wares, but under-
neath you subterranean misgivings ooze and threaten to wash away
your foundations. But with Wang Wei, it is different. He simply takes
his religion for granted, and goes on to practice it. He was a vegetarian,
and constantly resorted to the practice of Zen or Ch'an, which means
sitting silently and holding communion with the divine. As he says in
one of his poems:

*In the eventide, by the side of a crystal pool,*
*I practice ch'an to control the poisonous dragon in me.*

About thirty, he lost his wife, and he remained a widower for the rest of his days. But he kept two sweet mistresses, who were not only not jealous of each other, but mutually helpful—I mean poetry and painting! Besides being a great poet, he was also a famous painter. Su Tung-p'o used to say about him that "in his paintings there is poetry, and in his poems there is painting." For instance, what a beautiful picture he paints here:

## ON VISITING A VILLAGE

*As the sun casts its slanting rays upon a secluded village,*
*The returning cattle and sheep emerge at the end of a deep lane.*
*A rustic old man, waiting for his herd-boy to come home,*
*Stands leaning on his staff by the thatched door.*
*At the call of the whirring pheasants, the wheat is coming into ear.*
*As the silkworms sleep, the mulberry leaves are thinning.*
*Hoes on their shoulders, the farmers arrive one after another.*
*When they meet, they exchange cordial greetings.*
*Oh the charm of rural life, so simple and happy!*
*Filled with yearnings, I sing "'Tis Time to Return!"*

O dear Wang Wei! How you fill my heart with similar yearnings! When can I hear again "the soft gurgling music which I heard welling up from the sappy roots of the earth?" When can I see once more the "soft landscape of mild earth?"

*Where all was harmony, and calm, and quiet,*
*Luxuriant, budding; cheerful without mirth,*
*Which, if not happiness, is much more nigh it*
*Than your mighty passions.*

And what soothing images are evoked by this poem on "The Blue-green Stream":

*To enter the Yellow-flower River,*
*I start from the Green Streams.*
*A myriad turns along the hills*
*Cover barely a journey of thirty miles.*
*Rapids become noisy over heaped rocks:*
*Colors are crystallized in the thickets of pines.*

*The water-chestnuts sway gracefully on the waves:*
*The reeds are reflected in the water.*
*My heart, already at peace with itself,*
*Feels at home in the limpid stream.*
*Oh, to sit upon a rock and cast a fishing line!*
*Can there be a better way to spend the rest of my life?*

Not that he longs to escape from the world, but that he longs to live in the bosom of Mother Nature. How much at home he feels when he is alone with Nature is revealed in his poem on "The Bamboo Grove":

*Beneath the bamboo grove, alone,*
    *I seize my lute and sit and croon;*
*No ear to hear me, save my own,*
    *No eyes to see me, save the moon.*
Translated by GILES

To be seen by the moon is enough of a happiness to him. He is even more infatuated with Nature than Meng Hao-jan. When he is alone, he just plays the lute and enjoys himself, like a child on the lap of its mother. The mother says, "Look, look, my little baby! The moon is peeking at you!" and the baby is pleased. He does not feel, as Hao-jan does:

*I gaze upon my idle lute and sigh:*
    *Alas no sympathetic ear is near!*

Not is he like Rousseau on the Island of Saint-Pierre, who cried out in ecstasy, "O nature! O my mother! Behold me under thy protection alone! Here there is no knave to thrust himself between thee and me." He would rather say to Nature, "My little ma, I am so happy here! My ma, you must never leave me alone. But, my ma, when will you have another baby to play with me and share these candies with me?"

And Wang Wei does share his candies with his friends. In a beautiful letter, rendered into beautiful English by Arthur Waley, he invites Pei Ti to enjoy solitude together with him. I want to reproduce the letter here in Waley's translation, with a few alterations:

*This winter has been mild and comfortable, and it would be quite a pleasure to cross the mountain. But as you are conning the classics, I have hesitated to invite you over. So I have roamed about the mountain-side, rested at the Kan-p'ei Temple, dined with the monks, and, after dinner, resumed my roamings. Going northwards I crossed the old dam where the bright moon cast the image of the old castle in the waters. Later in the night I mounted the Hua-tzu Mound and watched the reflection of the moon tossed up and down by the waves and ripples of Wang River. Distant lights twinkled beyond the woods. In some deep lane a dog barked at the cold, with a cry like that of a leopard. The sound of villagers grinding their corn at night chimed with a distant bell.*

*Just now I am sitting all alone in my room; my servants have all gone to bed. My mind is filled with memories of the old days when we used to saunter forth hand in hand, composing poems as we went, and walking down the narrow paths we arrived at the banks of clear streams.*

*I am looking forward to the middle of Spring when the grasses will have grown and trees blossomed forth, and spring hills will be a real sight to see. What delight it will be to watch the young trout leaping from the stream, the white gulls stretching their wings, the green meadow sprinkled with dew, and the curlews announcing the dawn from the barley-fields! The time is drawing near, and may I expect you to come then to join me in enjoying the season? If I did not know your natural love for the ethereal, I would not have dared to send you an invitation of so little worldly importance. But I am sure you will find the visit deeply interesting. Please do come.*

Although conning the classics is important, enjoying Nature is even more so. The friend did accept the invitation, and came over to enjoy solitude together. He also wrote a charming poem on the bamboo grove:

> *In the bamboo grove of my friend,*
> *We grow daily more intimate with Nature.*
> *Far from the madding crowd,*
> *Only the mountain birds hobnob with us.*

Indeed, only a very noble person can enjoy Nature in the right mood. How this letter of Wang Wei's recalls to my mind a lovely letter my good friend Holmes wrote to me over twelve years ago from Beverly Farms:

*Also for two hours I drive and motor about this beautiful and interesting region, which I am sorry you did not see. One may gaze over lonely cliffs upon the seas or pass along smooth boulevards by crowded beaches, or skirt windswept downs and fine inland farms, or evoke the past by visiting houses built two centuries ago. That is not long for China, but it is long enough for romance. I say that all society is founded on the death of men. Certainly the romance of the past is. So much so that*

*the memorial tablets of a great war have the effect of two centuries added. I could
run on for a great while, but I must stop.*

Mr. T. K. Chuan once mentioned to me how natural and spontaneous Homes' style of writing seemed to him. I think it is because he was
such a great lover of Nature. And the style of Holmes is like that of
Wang Wei, because the touch of Nature makes them kin.

Another poem of Wang Wei, written in his fifties, I like very much:

## MY HOUSE ON CHUNG-NAN MOUNTAIN

*Since my middle age, I have taken to the cult of Tao,
But only lately have I been able to make my home by the hillside.
Whenever the spirit moves in me, I saunter forth all alone,
To feast my eyes and nurse my soul with the thrilling beauties of nature.
I walk along a water-course and follow it to its source;
I sit down and watch the clouds as they are just beginning to rise.
Sometimes when I chance upon an old fellow in the woods,
We would chat and smile and forget to return home.*

So he was not only a Buddhist, but also a Taoist. Probably, he was
not even aware of the difference between the two. Nor, indeed, am I. I
suspect that all genuine Chinese are fundamentally Taoistic in mental
outlook, whatever the religion they may adopt. Taoism is no religion,
but it is the way religions are received. In fact, as I have pointed out
elsewhere, the greatest statesmen in the history of China have been men
who acted like Confucians, but felt like Taoists. Recently, re-reading
Holmes' letters to me, I was thrilled to find that he too was at once a
Confucian and a Taoist! Who else could have written like this: "We
must be serious in order to get work done, but when the usual Saturday
half holiday comes I see no reason why we should not smile at the trick
by which Nature keeps us at our job. It makes me enormously happy
when I am encouraged to believe that I have done something of what
I should have liked to do, but in the subterranean misgivings I think, I
believe that I think sincerely, that it does not matter much." Now I
discover why I loved Holmes so much!

But to return to Wang Wei, what is the essence of the cult of Tao
that he spoke of? Listen to the words of Lao Tzu:

*But I alone am different from others in that I realize
the importance of feeding upon the Mother.*

It is natural for man to love Nature:

## AN ENCOUNTER

> *Sir, from my dear old home you come,*
> *And all its glories you can name;*
> *Oh tell me, has the winter-plum*
> *Yet blossomed o'er the window-frame?*
>                                   GILES' version

But is it less natural to love our friends? No, not for Wang Wei:

## OH TAKE ONE MORE CUP!

> *A morning shower has cleansed the dust from the city of Wei.*
> *The inn looks newly painted, and the willows are freshly green.*
> *Oh, take another cup of wine before you go away!*
> *Beyond this Pass of Yang no more old friends are to be seen!*

I cannot take leave of Wang Wei without referring to a beautiful poem called "Among Hills on an Autumnal Evening," which looks like some casual notes for a picture to be painted, but which contains two concluding lines whose meaning has grown upon me:

> *Windswept hills—after a fresh shower.*
> *The weather—Autumn in eventide.*
> *Bright moon shining through the pine trees.*
> *A clear stream flowing on pebbles.*
> *Bamboos noisy—washing maids returning.*
> *A stir among water-lilies—fishing boats starting.*
> *The Genius of Spring will stay with you for aye,*
> *If you don't mind too much its going away!*

To a spring poet, every season is Spring!

# THE PRINCE OF SPRING
## HIS LIFE

SPRING IS NOT ALWAYS as dulcet and calm as the poetry of Wang Wei. Speaking of Spring in New England, Mark Twain once said that he had counted one hundred and sixty-six different kinds of weather inside of twenty-four hours. I humbly submit that this is an exaggeration; but according to a Chinese proverb there are no less than eighteen changes in the course of a Spring day. In this sense, no one embodies the spirit of Spring more thoroughly than Li Po (701–762). A supreme romantic genius, a poet of the greatest variety of moods, he is a veritable "mingled yarn of joy and grief." But in order to appreciate his poetry to the fullest extent, we must know something of his life.

Like the wind that bloweth where it listeth, we do not know exactly when and where Li Po was born. The question of the time of his birth is easier to settle. For we know he died in 762, and we also know from a reliable source that he died in his sixty-second year (Chinese counting), so we can infer that he must have been born in 701. As to his birthplace, it has been a controversial subject for more than a millennium. Shantung, Kansu, Szechuen, and even Nanking have each claimed him for its own. Recently, it has been asserted with a great deal of plausibility that he first saw the light in the western part of Chinese Turkestan, that is, west of what is now known as Kansu. After carefully looking into the evidence, I feel pretty sure that this was the case. The fact seems to be this: By the end of the Shui Dynasty, that is, in the 610's, Li Po's ancestors, apparently for some crime, escaped incognito from their original home in Kansu westwards into the western part of

Chinese Turkestan. It was not until 705 that Li Keh, Li Po's father, moved his family secretly into Szechuen and settled in Chengtu. But at that time Li Po was already four years old.

Whatever the place of his birth, there is no question that he spent his childhood in Szechuen, famous for its gigantic mountains and wonderful natural scenery. We even know where he used to study his books, as may be gathered from a poem Tu Fu wrote in 761, when he was in Chengtu:

> I have not seen Li Po for a long time—
> What a pitiable man with his feigned madness!
> All the world wants to kill him:
> I alone dote on his genius.
> Quick-witted, he has hit off a thousand poems;
> A waif in the world, his only home is in a cup of wine.
> O my friend! 'Tis time to return to Ku'ang Shan,*
> Where you used to read books with such gusto.

But what did he read? Confucian classics, such as *The Book of Songs* and *The Book of History,* were, of course, among the things he took to heart. But, he liked even more to look into astrological and metaphysical books such as *Liu Chia* and *T'ai Hsuan Ching.* His interests were moreover not confined to mere book learning. A boy of infinite curiosity, he even learned the art of taming wild birds. Like Dr. Faustus, he tried his hand at one thing after another in rapid succession. "When I was fifteen," he said in an autobiographical letter, "I was fond of sword-play, and with that art I challenged quite a few great men." By the time he was twenty, he had killed with his own hands several persons, apparently for chivalrous causes. He had led a wild life, it is true; but he was by nature generous, and open-handed with his money. He had something of the knight-errant in him.

He did not leave Szechuen until he was in his middle twenties, when he sailed down the Yangtze, passing through the T'ung T'ing Lake, going as far as Nanking and Yangchow, and finally returning upstream to Yun Meng in Hupeh for a rest. His days of apprenticeship were done, and his days of wandering had begun. Although in Yun Meng he was married to a granddaughter of a retired Prime Minister by the name of Hsu Hsin-shih even marriage could not domesticate this wild

* Ku'ang Shan is a mountain lying near the city of Chengtu.

bird; for in 735 we find him in Shansi, where one of the most important events of his life happened. He met Kuo Tzu-i there, still serving in the ranks as a humble soldier, and saved him from a court-martial by speaking to the commander. Little did he know that Kuo was later to become saviour of the Empire and of his own life. But for this chivalrous act, the course of the history of T'ang would have been different. Could it be that Li Po intuitively saw even then some of the potentialities of this great soldier?

A little later, we find him in Shantung, entering into a warm friendship with five other men of letters. The six gentlemen, lovers of wine all, called themselves "Six Idlers of the Bamboo Brook."

But his wanderlust was insatiable. He went South, roaming the hills and floating on the rivers and lakes of Chekiang and Kiangsu. While in Shaohsin he became a friend of the famous Taoist priest Wu Yun. In 742, Wu Yun was summoned by Ming Huang to his court, and he spoke of Li Po very highly, so that his majesty was moved to invite the latter also to the capital. There Li Po met another Taoist, Ho Chih-chang, who was then serving in the court as a guest of the Crown Prince. On the very first meeting, Ho exclaimed, "Why, you do not belong to this world. You are an angel banished from Heaven." Li Po remained grateful to Chih-chang throughout his life. If, as Emerson said, "next to the originator of a good sentence is the first quoter of it," we can also say that next to a man of genius is the first man who recognizes him to the fullest extent. "An angel banished from Heaven!"

That was exactly what Li Po thought himself to be! Had his mother not dreamed, on the eve of his birth, of a star falling from the skies? At any rate, the two poets took to each other at first sight. Chih-chang took a gold tortoise he was wearing around the waist, as a badge of official honor, and exchanged it for wine, and the two new friends had a jolly time. Some days later Li Po was given an audience in the Palace of Golden Bells, and expounded his views on current politics fluently and, we may believe, sensibly, for Ming Huang was so delighted with him that he treated him to a grand banquet, "seasoning the soup for him personally," as history says. It is also recorded that Li Po had knowledge of some "barbarian language"—I am sure it was not English, as it was almost three centuries before Beowulf saw the light—and drafted for Ming Huang some diplomatic document in that language. History stops with this meager information, but it is the foundation upon which an interesting story is built, which has been translated by E. R. Howell as "The Diplomacy of Li Tai-po."

Li Po seemed on the way to a great political career but he was very fond of wine. Soon he became a prominent member of a group called "The Eight Immortals of the Wine-cup," including among others his bosom friend Chih-chang. If Chih-chang was topsy-turvy, Li Po was inside out. Of him Tu Fu says:

> Li Po produces a hundred poems before he has finished a peck of wine
> He sleeps in a wine shop at Ch'ang-an market-place.
> When the Son of Heaven summons him, he does not board the boat;
> "Does His Majesty know," he says, "that his humble servant is a drunken angel?"

In reality he was not so bad as Tu Fu caricatured him, but he was bad enough. Once (in 744) Ming Huang wanted him to draft some imperial edicts, and sent someone to fetch him. He did go, but he was drunk, and cold water had to be sprinkled on his face before he became aware of what he was doing. As soon as he took the brush, however, he wrote without interruption and finished the writing at one sitting. On another occasion, he was requested to write some songs in praise of the beautiful Yang Kuei-fei, to be set to music by the famous musician Li Kuei-nien. At the suggestion of the Emperor that he take off his heavy boots and use light shoes, he stretched out his feet to the powerful eunuch Kao Lih-shih, who was serving His Majesty and not Li Po, and bade him pull off his boots. Kao, of course. had to do it, but he never forgave him for this insult. And no one can blame Kao for being offended, because eunuchs as a rule are preys to an inferiority complex. In one of the three songs Li Po wrote on that occaion, he compared Yang Kuei-fei to "Flying Swallow Chao," one of the most beautiful but unscrupulous queens in the Han Dynasty, who suffered a tragic end. He might have done it with or without malice. At any rate, Kao, who was still writhing under a fresh insult, readily saw the innuendo, and called Kuei-fei's attention to it. Kuei-fei at first was overjoyed at the praise, as a fat lady must be when made to believe she was as light as a "flying swallow," but was finally convinced that it was a dig at her, and thenceforth did her best to prevent any further promotion of the haughty poet. I only wonder whether Kuei-fei thought of that poetic prophecy when twelve years later she met a tragic death.

Li Po, with all his political ambitions, was not a man meant for the court. Ming Huang, who wavered for a time between the love of genius and the love of beauty, finally yielded to the latter, and decided to get rid of the unruly horse by politely sending him away with generous gifts of gold and silver. The wild horse went away, and formally became a Taoist. He made his home in Shantung, but he traveled far and wide in the next ten years, covering almost all the provinces, and I suspect that most of his Nature-poems were written during this period. But in 755, An Lu-shan rebelled; Ming Huang had to escape into Szechuen; in the next year, the Crown Prince assumed the reins of government without the consent of Ming Huang; and Prince Ling of Yung, Ming Huang's sixteenth son, contemplating a declaration of independence from the new monarch, invited Li Po to join him as an advisor. Unfortunately for Li Po, the troops of Prince Ling were routed in 757, and our poet had to escape to P'eng Tse in Kiangsi, but was caught and put in prison. He was sentenced to death, but Kuo Tzu-i, whom he had saved twenty years before, and who was by this time the Minister of War and the commander-in-chief of the imperial troops, went to the new Emperor and offered to ransom the life of Li Po by giving up his own official rank. Incidentally, Kuo Tzu-i, the greatest soldier-statesman of T'ang, was a Nestorian, and in this case he certainly showed the spirit of Christ. As a result of his intercession, the death sentence was remitted, and instead Li Po was banished to Yeh Lang. Before he reached Yeh Lang, however, he was pardoned and returned to Kiangsi. In his latter years, his travels were confined mainly to Nanking and two cities in Anhui: Hsuan Ch'eng and Li Yang.

According to a report, which Herbert Giles accepted as a historical fact, Li Po "was drowned on a journey, from leaning one night too far over the edge of a boat in a drunken effort to embrace the reflection of the moon." The story is beautiful, but not true, for in 762, the poet's friend Li Yang-ping became magistrate of Tang T'u in Szechuen, and he went to join him there. He was appointed by Tai Tsung, who had just ascended the throne, to be a censor, the first time he was ever named to a governmental office. But when the order of appointment reached Szechuen, Li Po had already died.

Many critics have said that Li Po led an easy life and that his poetry is mostly hedonistic. As if it were not tragedy enough to be a man of

genius! To be a man of genius is to be hypersensitive. I think Li Po
would agree with Chesterton that "Death is more tragic even than
death by starvation," and that "Having a nose is more comic than having a Mormon nose." To be a man of genius is to be a possessed man;
Li Po was possessed by the Muse, but he also had a strong desire for
action, which was bound to be frustrated in spite of his ambitions. In
this connection, some remarks by Walter Raleigh on Shakespeare seem
to be relevant to the case of Li Po, thus I quote them at some length:

*But the central drama of his mind is the tragedy of the life of imagination. He was
a lover of clear decisive action, and of the deed done. He knew and condemned the
sentiment which fondly nurses itself and is without issue. Yet, on the other hand,
the gift of imagination with which he was so richly dowered, the wide, restless,
curious searchings of the intelligence and the sympathies—these faculties, strong in
him by nature, and strengthened every day by the exercise of his profession, bade
fair at times to take sole possession, and to paralyse the will. Then he revolted
against himself, and was almost inclined to bless that dark, misfeatured messenger
called the angel of this life, "whose care is lest men see too much at once." If for the
outlook of a god the seer must neglect the opportunities and duties of a man, may not
the price paid be too high? It is a dilemma known to all poets,—to all men, indeed,
who live the exhausting life of the imagination, and grapple hour by hour, in
solitude and silence, with the creatures of their mind, while the passing invitation
of humanity, which never recur are ignored or repelled.*

*Keats knew the position well, and has commented on it, though not tragically, in
some passages of his letters. "Men of Genius," he says, "are great as certain ethereal
chemicals operating on the mass of neutral intellect—but they have not any in-
dividuality, any determined character." And again: "A poet is the most unpoetical
of anything in existence, because he has no Identity—he is continually in for and
filling some other body." Keats also recognised, as well as Shakespeare, that man
cannot escape the call to action, and it was he who said—"I am convinced more and
more, every day, that fine writing is, next to fine doing, the top thing in the world."
But what if this highest call came suddenly, as it always does, and finds the man
unnerved and unready, given over to "sensations and day-nightmares," absorbed
in speculation, out of himself, and unable to respond? A famous English painter was
once, at his own request, bound to the mast during a storm at sea, in order that he
might study the pictorial effects of sky and water. His help was not wanted in the
working of the ship; he was not one of the crew. Who among men, in the conduct of
his own life, dare claim a like exemption?*

# THE PRINCE OF SPRING
## HIS POETRY

IF WANG WEI IS MELODIOUS, Li Po is symphonic. It seems as though the Spring of T'ang Poetry would not come to close without having an appropriate finishing canter, without having someone to recapitulate all its phases. For Li Po is as full of gladness and free of heaven as Wang Fan-chih; almost as boastful and self-confident as Tu Shen-yen, only more justifiably so; as strong in creative impulse and cosmic emotion as Ch'en Tzu-ang and Chang Jo-hsu, only with better results; as keen and subtle in his understanding of the psychology of women as Wang Ch'ang-ling or any other "chamber poets": and finally he has produced word-pictures comparable in beauty, though of a different kind, to those of Wang Wei and Meng Hao-jan. Let us follow him in all these phases roughly in the order mentioned. The following lines recall to mind the voice of Fan-chih:

> *We drank continuously and finished a hundred jugs,*
> *Till our minds were rinsed clean of ageless sorrows.*
> *An ideal night it was to engage in transcendental talks,*
> *For the clear moonlight would not let us go to bed.*
> *Feeling drowsy at last, we slept in the open hills,*
> *With the sky for blanket and the earth for pillow.*

Li Po's haughtiness is well-known. He was conscious of it himself, and he suffered a great deal for it. As he said:

> *Men of the world all sneer at my high talks,*
> *Which are not attuned to their ears.*

How unpopular he became in his lifetime is testified to by Tu Fu:

> *All the world wants to kill him:*
> *I alone dote on his genius.*

"To be great is to be misunderstood," as Emerson puts it, and Li Po forms no exception to the rule. Probably, the chief reason why he was misunderstood was that in his mind this world, which we ordinary folks take so seriously, is nothing but an empty dream. As he says:

> *I am haughty to the world, and slight its transient glories.*
> *Not that I harbor no practical plans in my bosom;*
> *But that I make a jest of all the heroes in history,*
> *And regard all their deeds as children's plays.*

Even the Universe itself will not stay forever:

> *The sun and the moon will eventually pass away;*
> *Heaven and Earth will some day rot and decay.*
> *The insects that nest in a green pine and sing*
> *Think this tree must be an immutable thing.*

An insect himself, he looks at the world with the eyes of an angel. When he was in Huchow, a magistrate asked who he was, and he blurted out:

> *A scholar of Green Lotus,*
> *I have been called an immortal in exile.*
> *For thirty years I have led*
> *A hidden life in wine shops.*
> *O, you Prefect of Hu-chou, why must you*
> *Ask about my origins?*
> *I am none other than a reincarnation*
> *Of the ancient Buddha of golden grains.*

That he doesn't regard himself as belonging to this world is revealed by another poem:

> *You ask what my soul does away in the sky,*
> *I inwardly smile but cannot reply;*
> *Like the peach-blossom carried away by the stream,*
> *I soar to a world of which you cannot dream.*
>
> GILES' version

I should imagine that Li Po sometimes felt as Shakespeare did:

> *Man, proud man,*
> *Drest in a little brief authority,*
> *Most ignorant of what he is most assur'd,*
> *His glassy essence, like an angry ape,*
> *Plays such fantastic tricks before high heaven*
> *As make the angels weep.*

One of the reasons I like Li Po so much is the iconoclastic tendency that I find in him; for one has to tear down all the idols before one can worship the living God!

But the pathetic thing about Li Po is that, since he doesn't belong to this world, he must find some other world to belong to. His plight is, indeed, like that of "a sea animal living on land, wanting to fly in the air." Like Ch'en Tzu-ang, he wanted to enter the gate of immortality on the chariot of mutation! This explains his insatiable wanderlust and cosmic yearnings. This explains also his continuous effort to seek for the happiness of insensibility by getting soddenly drunk.

Some poems of Li Po remind me of the drawing by William Blake called "I Want! I Want!" in which, as the reader will recall, a man is just beginning to climb a long ladder spanning the earth and the moon. For instance these lines:

> *The ancients didn't see the moon of tonight,*
> *But the moon did shine upon the ancients.*
> *The past and the present form a flowing stream,*
> *Upon whose endless ripples the moon reflects its light eternally.*
>
>       \*     \*     \*
>
> *Let me lay down my cup for a moment and ask:*
> *O Sky! Since how long did you have the moon?*
> *I want to climb up to the bright moon, but I can't;*
> *And yet the moon never ceases to follow me as I walk!*

In this connection, I reproduce a piece as translated by L. Cranmer-Byng:

### DRIFTING

> *We cannot keep the gold of yesterday;*
>   *Today's dun clouds we cannot roll away.*
> *Now the long, wailing flight of geese brings autumn in its train,*
> *So to the view-tower cup in hand to fill and drink again.*

And dream of the great singers of the past,
Their fadeless lines of fire and beauty cast.
I too have felt the wild-bird thrill of song behind the bars,
But these have brushed the world aside and walked amid the stars.
In vain we cleave the torrent's thread with steel,
In vain we drink to drown the grief we feel,
When man's desire with fate doth war thus, this avails alone
To hoist the sail and let the gale and the waters bear us on.

On rare occasions, he got a temporary illusion of having flown beyond this stifling universe, as in this:

In early morn I climb up the mountain-top,
I lift my hands to open the gate of clouds.
My spirit soars, expanding itself into the air,
Until it's gone beyond the sky and earth.

But most of the time he was aware that this endeavour to enter the gate of immutability on the chariot of mutation was doomed to failure, and so he took to wine in order to dull the edge of sensibility.

No long rope can tie the running sun—
All ages share this great sorrow in common.
Had I the yellow metal piled up to the stars,
I should use it to buy youth and fun.
A little spark of fire from the stone—
That is life in this world.
A moment past is a dream done;
What will become of us later is known to none.
Tell me not that you are too poor to drink,
Let us get wine and call our neighbors to our feast.
I doubt if there are immortals in the world,
But we can find sure happiness in the wine at least.

While some may have drunk more wine than Li Po, no one has written more poems about wine. Here is a charming defense of drinking:

If Heaven does not love wine,
Then the star of wine would not be in Heaven.
If Earth does not love wine,
Then the fountain of wine ought not to be on Earth.
Since Heaven and Earth both love wine,
Then to love wine is worthy of God.

*When clear, wine is comparable to a saint:*
*When turgid, a learned savant.*
*Since you can drink and still remain a saint or a savant,*
*Then what is the use of becoming a god or a fairy?*
*Three cups open the door to the great way;*
*A peck brings you back to the bosom of Nature.*
*O, what infinite charms I find in wine!*
*To impart them to the sober is to cast pearls before swine.*

Thomas Fuller has said that "wine turns a man inside outwards." But everything depends upon the quality of what is inside the man. If he is at bottom a fool, then it would be wiser for him not to drink. But if he happens to be a man of genius, wine helps to evoke the best in him. In fact, one of the most famous songs of Li Po is "The Song of Wine," to whose throbbing music and yeasty madness no translation can ever do justice:

*Don't you see the waters of the Yellow River come from the skies,*
*And run endlessly toward the Ocean, ne'er to return?*
*Don't you see in the bright mirror in the high hall our white hairs*
*make a sorry scene?*
*In the morning they look like black silk: in the evening they become*
*snow!*
*In life, when you are happy, you must drink your joy to the last drop,*
*And don't let your gold goblets face the moon without wine!*
*Heaven has endowed me with genius, and will find a use for it:*
*As for money, a thousand pieces of gold scattered away will return*
*some day.*
*Let us roast a lamb and slay an ox and start the music!*
*We shall drink, each of us, three hundred cups of wine.*
*You Master Ts'en, and you Tan-ch'iu dear!*
*To you I offer wine, and refuse me not!*
*I'll sing a song for you. Please incline your ears and listen!*
*Bells and drums and choice dishes are not what I prize:*
*My only wish—to remain drunk and ne'er to be sober.*
*The sages and savants of old, who remember them now?*
*But the names of drunkards have resounded throughout all times.*
*Don't you remember the Prince of Ch'en how he used to feast in his*
*Palace of Peace and Pleasure?*
*What jolly and riotous times they had over endless measures of precious*
*liquors!*

*Why should my host worry about his poverty?*
*Let us order more wine, and I'll drink to you.*
*Look! What nice roan horses and costly furs you have!*
*Ask the boy to take them away and barter them for sweet wine!*
*Let us drown in wine the sorrows of ten thousand ages!*

And what sober man could have hit off things like this:

### A BOATING SONG

*A boat of spice-wood with oars of magnolia!*
*At both ends sit musicians with their flutes and golden pipes.*
*With a cask of good wine and such fair singers,*
*I let the waves carry me where they will.*
*Fairy on earth, I wait only to ride on the yellow crane.*
*Roamer of the seas, I have no mind to follow the white gulls.*
*The songs of Chu Ping are still shining like sun and moon:*
*The palaces of the Chu kings leave no trace in the hills.*
*When I burn with inspiration, my pen shakes the Five Mountains.*
*When my poem is done, I laugh the whole world to scorn.*
*Can worldly pomps and riches last forever?*
*As well to expect the Han River to flow westwards to its source!*

From the foregoing examples, it might seem that Li Po is an expressionist. He is that, but at times he can be extremely impressionistic, as in this:

### TEARS

*A fair girl draws the blind aside*
　　*And sadly sits with drooping head;*
*I see her burning tear-drops glide*
　　*But know not why those tears are shed.*
　　　　　　　　　　　GILES' version

This little piece has drawn a very sensible comment from Lytton Strachey: "The blind is drawn aside for a moment, and we catch a glimpse of a vision which starts us off on a mysterious voyage down the widening river of imagination." In fact, all his descriptions of women are impressionistic. Here is another lovely snapshot:

*A little maiden is gathering lotus on the brook of Yah.*
*Spying a passer-by, she turns her boat around, still continuing her song.*
*She disappears giggling into the thicket of lotus.*
*Pretending to be bashful, she hides herself among the flowers.*

He even wrote some charming lines for his wife meant to be presented to himself:

*I am like a peach flower in a well,*
*Blowing and smiling unseen.*
*My lord is like the moon on the sky—*
*When will he turn his gaze into this hidden place?*

Incidentally, we see what a negligent husband Li Po must have been. To be the wife of a poet is bad enough, but when the poet happens to be also a drunkard, I should imagine it's Hell. But our poet is not entirely without conscience. He is at least capable of laughing at himself. In a poem to his wife, he confessed his sins of omission:

*Throughout all the days of the years,*
*I am drunk as the mud.*
*Ah! to be T'ai-po's wife*
*Is to taste single blessedness to the full!*

His snapshots of Nature have some illusive quality about them. He just reproduces his immediate impressions, in which the objective and the subjective are mingled together like chemical compounds. Take this one:

*A dog barks through the crooning of the waters.*
*The peach blossoms are deep dyed in the rain.*
*Among the thick woods I catch occasional glimpses of deer.*
*The brooklet seems to slumber in the noontide, and no bells are heard.*
*The wild bamboos nick and notch the azure sky.*
*A fall hangs from a green cliff.*
*Nobody knows where the Taoist has gone.*
*I lean against one pine after another with my heart full of longings.*

Some of his word-pictures almost seem to anticipate the theory of relativity for they make you feel as though the earth were constantly falling to the apples instead of the other way round.

*Above the man's face arise the hills;*
*Besides the horse's head emerge the clouds.*

LIN YUTANG's version

\*          \*          \*

*The wild swans beckon the sorrowing heart away.*
*The mountain, bird-like, picks up the lovely moon in its beak.*

WEN YUAN-NING's version

But I like this best of all:

*Fragrant mists ooze all over the mountain,*
*Showers of flowers fall from the sky.*

For it transforms the earth into Heaven, making me think of St. Teresa's sweet *pluie de fleurs!*

Some Chinese critics have regarded Li Po as an egoist, as a man of genius with little human feeling. This does not strike me as a fair judgment. No one can deny his remarkable capacity for friendship. Who could, for instance, be more generous than he was:

### TO A FRIEND IN DISTRESS

*Your horse was yellow,*
*And mine was white.*
*But our hearts were equally mellow,*
*Differ as the colours of our horses might!*
*What a grand time we had together,*
*Racing around the suburbs of Loyang,*
*Wearing a dazzling sword each like the other,*
*Flaunting our head-gears all along.*
*Guests of the great, and not meanly dressed either,*
*Our life was like a long carefree song.*
*Now like a tiger you writhe entrapped—*
*A fate common to the heroic and strong.*
*When my bosom friend in distress is enwrapped,*
*I feel like a lost sheep not knowing where to belong.*

His profound sympathy for the oppressed is revealed by some of his songs exalting the virtues of the gallant people who would take others' injuries as personal insults and avenge them of their own accord. In this connection, I may mention that the cult of chivalry is an old tradition in China. The idea that we should only bow to the humble and soft, and never to the proud and oppressive, is bred in the bone of our people. Long before Confucius was born, songs had been sung in praise of chivalrous persons. This is from *The Book of Songs*:

> There is a common saying:
> "Chew the soft, spit out the hard."
> Chung-shan Fu acts differently:
> He neither chews the soft nor spits out the hard.
> For he would never oppress the poor and needy
> Or fear the powerful and haughty.

But the interesting thing is that this tradition of chivalry has been kept alive throughout the ages, not by the so-called "gentlemen," but principally by simple folks unspoiled by bookish learning. This seems to be the theme of one of Li Po's best known ballads:

> Look at the Knight of Chao!
> On his head a Tartar's cap,
> On his side a scimitar gleaming like snow,
> Seated on a silver saddle,
> Which adds a sheen to the white horse,
> He rides forth like a shooting star!
> Killing a man at every ten paces,
> He makes a thousand miles at a single stretch.
> When his mission is carried out,
> He shakes his garments and departs,
> Leaving no trace of his name,
> Or where he makes his home.
>
> Occasionally he stops at Hsin-ling's house,
> Laying his sword across the knees, he drinks.
> He cuts a piece of toast meat for Chu Hai,
> Offers a goblet of wine to Hou Ying.
> After three cups he utters a vow
> Weightier than the Five Mountains.
> When his eyes are dizzy and his ears hot,
> His heroic spirit blazes forth like clear rainbow.
> With a golden hammer he saves the kingdom of Chao,
> And the whole city of Han Tan lies trembling under his feet.
> The glory of two such heroes of old still shines,
> After a thousand years, over the ramparts of Ta Liang!

*Though dead, the fragrance of their chivalrous bones*
*Gives an undying tribute to the ideal of Manhood.*
*Who, then, can be contented to bury his head in his study,*
*Wasting a whole life over the dusty volumes of a* Tai Hsuan Ching?

No, Li Po was no cock-eyed pacifist. But he did not approve of wars of aggression either.

*In the battlefields men fight and die;*
*Their horses neigh piteously to Heaven.*
*Ravens and kites peck at their entrails;*
*They carry them away and hand them on the withered twigs.*
*The desert is smeared with the blood of men,*
*And what have the generals accomplished?*
*Oh nefarious war! I see why the sages of old*
*Would only resort to it when they were forced to it.*

After reading this, the reader will agree with me that it is unfair to charge Li Po with callousness to human suffering. It should, however, be admitted that his sympathy with mankind is not so warm and intimate as that of Tu Fu, and that there is always a barrier between this man of genius and the world at large. Somehow, Li Po looks at the human world as an anthill. He wrote, for instance:

*Dimly, the battlefield merges with yellow dusk;*
*The fighting men look like a swarm of ants.*

But Tu Fu looks at an anthill as a human world:

*I want to build a farm, but I pity the ants in the holes.*
*I wink at the poor village boys picking up the ears of grain.*

In other words, when Li Po deals with human subjects, I miss "the fierce electric high light"—to use an expression of Holmes—that I find in some of Tu Fu's poems.

It has always seemed to me Li Po is cosmically-minded, while Tu Fu is historically-minded. If I may be allowed to use some pompous terms in philosophy, I would say that the former is transcendental, while the latter is immanent. To take a homely instance, Li Po wrote the following poem "To a Firefly" when he was a mere child:

*Rain cannot quench thy lantern's light,*
*Wind makes it shine more brightly bright;*
*Once thou fly to heaven afar,*
*Thou'lt twinkle near the moon—a star!*
                                    GILES' version

So he attributed cosmic yearnings even to a firefly! Compare this with Tu Fu's lines on the same subject:

*Dancing round the well, each firefly calls forth a new partner from the deep;*
*Flying by the flowers, they send sudden flashes into the glories hidden in the dark.*

In one case, the firefly has to fly to heaven in order to acquire significance. In the other case, it can be significant even on earth. To my mind, unless we make our earth heavenly, Heaven itself will remain earthy.

Why, then, is Li Po significant? What entitles him to be ranked with the greatest poets, not only of China, but of the world? If, as he said, Heaven had given him genius and would find some use for it, we may be allowed to inquire what type of genius he is and what is its use.

To my mind, Li Po's significance lies in this: he is the most perfect embodiment of the spirit of romanticism. In life as well as in letters, he is a great romantic. Imaginative, passionate, contemptuous of form and convention, grandiose and picturesque in thought and language, remote from experience, and visionary—there is no romantic quality that he lacks. Whether you like him or not depends a great deal upon you own temperament. Being realistically inclined, I cannot help preferring Tu Fu to Li Po both as a man and a poet; but it would be worse than silly to deny that romanticism has its uses, especially for the present world. In his fine book on *The Decline and Fall of the Romantic Ideal*, F. L. Lucas says: "In this factory-world, whose walls we are daily building higher and higher round us, we are in danger of feeling more and more like mice in some vast generating-station; of forgetting that men remain more remarkable than anything men have made. . . . The individual needs new armour against the world; new foundations for the Ivory Tower of his own thought, the one sure reality, among these vibrations of a million wheels." In fact, the universe itself is apparently a big factory, with an infinite number of wheels eternally running and

revolving, and producing all forms of living beings that make their
appearance and struggle with one another for a brief moment and go
their way. Our earth itself is but a mouse in a vast generating-station,
and we are all microscopic parasites. To relieve ourselves a little from
the crushing sense of inferiority, it is good to be able to feel at times as
Li Po did:

> When I am inspired, I shake the Five Mountains with my pen!
> I challenge the earth and laugh it to scorn, as I rise on the wings of
>     Poesy!
>
> *       *       *
>
> In the midst of wine the cup of my joy is running over;
>     I hardly know it's midnight.
> I drink to your health, Emperor Yao, do you hear me?
>     Why don't you order Kao Yao to take up a comet,
> To make a clean sweep of the eight corners of the Cosmos,
>     And rid us once for all of these brooding clouds?

In the meantime, clouds are still brooding, and the world is not to be
improved by an angel beating ineffectually against the void. But it
would be worse to allow vacant-minded persons to beat effectually
against an angel. For romanticism can at least impart a ferment, although it furnishes no program for action.

It is because Li Po is a great romantic that in his hands everything becomes so fast moving and quickened with life. One imagines that even
his white hair grows rampant like the wild grass in Spring:

### ON HIS WHITE HAIR

> Methinks my white hair has grown ten thousand feet long!
> For it grows alongside of my sorrow.
> I only wonder how all this autumn frost
> Has entered into the bright mirror in front of me.

And take this description of a journey:

### I LEFT THE CITY OF PO TI AT DAWN

> At early dawn I left Po Ti among the many-colored clouds.
> Now I find myself back in Chiang-ling—a thousand li in the course of
>     a day!

*The monkeys had hardly done with their continuous howlings on the*
  *shores*
*Before ten thousand ranges of hills had rolled away from my light skiff!*

If the reader compares this with Wang Wei's

*Following the hills, making ten thousand turnings;*
*We go rapidly, but advance scarcely a hundred li.*

he will find how very different the temperaments of the two poets are.
Li Po is glad to have covered a great distance in a short time, but Wang
Wei is glad to have advanced only a short distance in a long time. It
seems to me that Li is at his best in painting Nature in her dynamic
aspects, while Wang is at his best in painting her in her restful and calm
moods.

Some of Li Po's word-pictures possess a sweep peculiarly his own;
for instance, here is what he says about the fall at Lushan:

*Flying straight down three thousand feet,*
*It looks as if the Milky Way had fallen from the sky!*

And I don't remember either Wang Wei or Tu Fu as having ever
written this way:

*Tonight I stay at the Summit Temple*
*I feel I can touch the stars by lifting my hands*
*I dare not speak aloud for fear*
*Of disturbing the blessed in Heaven.*

       \*       \*       \*

*The sea does not fill up my retina;*
*How can its waves satisfy my heart?*

       \*       \*       \*

*The Yellow River falls from the skies and runs eastward into the seas.*
*Ten thousand li of water pours itself into my bosom!*

       \*       \*       \*

*God the Supreme Artist painted the City of Chengtu,*
*And all the houses and gates enter into His canvas!*

       \*       \*       \*

*Like a silken thread, the Yellow River flows at the border of heaven.*

       \*       \*       \*

*The two rivers look like a pair of bright mirrors inlaid in the land.*
*The twin bridges hang before us like a gorgeous rainbow.*

*My sorrow follows the stream till it lengthens into ten thousand li!*

        \*       \*       \*

*Look, look! How lovely, yonder River of Han, green as a duck's head!*
*Exactly like grape-wine in its first stage of fermentation!*

        \*       \*       \*

*Men are walking in a bright mirror.*
*Birds pass in and out through a beautiful screen.*

From a "Song on a Crystal Brook"

In other words, Li Po looks at Nature as an endless scroll of pictures. On the other hand, he looks at a picture as a natural scene:

*The great artist has spun his subtle thoughts and brandished his*
    *gorgeous brush,*
*Driving the mountains and whipping the oceans to come before our eyes!*

        \*       \*       \*

*It looks as though the twelve peaks of Wu-shan*
*Had flown from Heaven's border into your silken screen!*

Sometimes, even the feathered songsters wish to chime in with human music:

*Our music has thrilled the hearts of new nightingales.*
*They have flown over, to the trees in the Royal Park.*
*Hark! They too have begun to pipe, mingling their notes*
*With the glorious concert of flutes and fifes!*

Anyone who has heard a caged bird burst into song in the evening when he turns on the radio cannot fail to feel the fundamental unity of God's creation. One heart is throbbing throughout the expanding universe! Li Po goes as far as to say:

*If you know the heart of the dodder and the vine,*
*You would be able to measure the tides of the sea!*

How this flash of insight reminds me of a few lines from Tennyson, otherwise so different from Li Po:

*Flower in the crannied wall,*
*I pluck you out of the crannies,*
*I hold you here, root and all, in my hand,*
*Little flower—but if I could understand,*

*What you are, root and all, and all in all,*
*I should know what God and man is.*

The web of life is so closely interwoven that all things are but the modes of one substance:

*Chuang Chow dreamed of a butterfly,*
*And the butterfly was Chuang Chow!*
*One reality is constantly changing its forms:*
*Endless events are flowing into eternity!*

Is it not because of this wonderful inter-relatedness of God's creation that even now, as I am writing this, tears have suddenly gushed into my eyes again when I think of the soldiers at the front. Their blood has changed into my tears! In the meantime, Summer has arrived. So good-bye, reader, I can write no more!

*Ah! such romantic soarings,*
*Such restlessness and curvetting!*
*Where will all this heroism lead to?*

This sounds more like a man chiding a boy than a young fellow addressing a friend twelve years his senior! On the other hand, Li Po presented an equally impolite poem to Tu Fu:

*I met Tu Fu on the tops of the Rice Hill,*
*Wearing a big bamboo hat under the noontide sun.*
*How is it you have grown so very thin?*
*You must have put too much bitter efforts into the making of poetry!*

This sounds like a precocious boy having a naughty dig at an elder. A friend of mine has given a delightfully idiomatic turn to the two lines:

*Gee! You are losing weight terribly!*
*Maybe your poems have got all the weight you have lost!*

Neither Li nor Tu seemed to be aware that they belonged to different seasons, that Spring, newly liberated as it was from the grip of death into a new being, was bound to suffer a dizzy agony in its sheer metempsychosis, while Summer was bound to be heavy with the luxuriant process of aestivation and ripening. The truth is Li Po's lyrics are delightful, but their tantalizing effect is momentary. Tu Fu's are not so light at the first reading, but they sink deep down in your psyche. To me Tu Fu was decidedly the greater genius of the two. He possessed the highest artistic talent without the drawback of an artistic temperament.

In fact, the poetry of T'ang was so much of an organism and followed its stages of development so inevitably that the poets in its first stage look like little children in comparison with a man like Tu Fu. For instance, Tu Shen-yen was the grandfather of Tu Fu, but from the standpoint of poetic maturity Tu Fu may be regarded as the grandfather. Shen-yen died in his sixties, and his last words were: "That little kid the Creator is doing his best to harass me! What more can I say?" Tu Fu died in his fifties, and his last poem, written after an attack of paralysis, contains these significant lines:

*Like a clear level mirror, I have been a fool who knows not how to*
*flatter.*
*Verily, the light of God has illumined and guided me in my journey*
*through life.*

Shen-yen was trying to be funny like a naughty boy, but Tu Fu achieved real humour through a high seriousness. And who was the grandfather?

At any rate, we have to thank Spring for all its charms and all its innocent prattles, but the year would not be complete without the other seasons, and just now we have to deal with Summer. For reasons of time and space I shall confine myself to Tu Fu, the Soul of Summer.

The most prominent quality of Summer is its heat. Corresponding to this aspect of the season is the intense fire of love burning incessantly in the heart of Tu Fu. He loves God and all His creatures except the vultures preying upon others. The scope of his never-dying sympathy ranges from the emperor to the commonest grass on the wayside. He writes scathing satires against the perpetrators of social injustice and heartless cruelty precisely because he has so much affection for their innocent victims. In other words, his very hate gathers momentum from his all-embracing love. For it is not beyond human possibilities to love one's personal enemies, but who can ever help hating the enemies of God? Among the worst enemies of God are the war-makers, whom Tu Fu hates with the intensity of his love for humanity. Here is how he paints a recruiting scene:

> Chariots rumble! Horses neigh!
> Each with a bow and arrows at his girdle, the footmen are ready to go
>     their way!
> Their fathers, mothers, wives and children have come to bid them adieu;
> The crowd has raised a confusion of dust, till the bridge is shut off from
>     view.
> They clutch at the men's clothes; they stamp their feet; they cry on the
>     roads,
> Till the echoes of their piteous wailings rise to the clouds.

To Tu Fu's mind, all this misery which turned the earth into hell was uncalled for. He laid the blame at the door of the emperor, whose lust for territories knew no bounds.

> The frontiers have become an ocean of blood.
> But the war-minded Emperor is still bent upon expanding the empire.
> Does His Majesty know that two hundred districts east of the mountain
>     are lying waste,

*And all the villages, big and small, are overgrown with briars and thorns?*

The earth exists to feed men with its fruits, but when things are not what they ought to be, men exist to feed the earth with their blood. Ming Huang already possessed more land than he had men to cultivate; but he continued to draw the farmers from their fields to the remote frontiers. That was what Tu Fu could not understand.

*Is His Majesty not rich enough in territories?*
*Why open up still more frontiers?*

And as if it were not enough to deprive wives of their husbands, fathers of their sons, and children of their fathers, the government continued to levy all sorts of taxes, duties and rents upon the poverty-stricken families. "Where," Tu Fu asks without waiting for an answer, "where can they get money to meet these exactions?"

The following specimens will give a glimpse into the social conditions brought about directly or indirectly by the wars:

## THE SONG OF SILKWORMS AND COWS

*In the world, there are nearly ten thousand cities,*
 *But ah! what a pity*
*That weapons of war and soldiers fill up*
 *Each and every city!*
*When will the swords and shields be beaten*
 *Into hoes and ploughs,*
*So every inch of waste land may be tilled*
 *By the patient cows?*
  *Cows till the mow,*
  *And silkworms grow!*
*Farmers and silk-maids sing as they go!*
*Tears of passionate scholars cease to flow!*
  *   *   *   *   *
*Last year the price of rice was high,*
 *And the soldiers had not enough to eat.*
*This year the price of rice is low,*
 *And the farmers can't make both ends meet.*
*The great officials, riding high horses,*
 *Are overfed with wine and meat;*

*In the farmers' barns no grain is left,*
    *And on their looms, of silk there's not a sheet!*
            * * * * *

*Everywhere the poor are selling their children*
*In order to pay their rents and taxes.*
            * * * * *

*Over the earth so wide and waste,*
*I see few men, but many vultures!*
            * * * * *

## THE PRESSGANG

*There, where at eve I sought a bed,*
    *A pressgang came, recruits to hunt;*
*Over the wall the goodman sped,*
    *And left his wife to bear the brunt.*

*Ah me! the cruel serjeant's rage!*
    *Ah me! how sadly she anon*
*Told all her story's mournful page,—*
    *How three sons to the war had gone;*

*How one had sent a line to say*
    *That two had been in battle slain:*
*He, from the fight had run away,*
    *But they could ne'er come back again.*

*She swore 'twas all the family—*
    *Except a grandson at the breast;*
*His mother too was there, but she*
    *Was all in rags and tatters drest.*

*The crone with age was troubled sore,*
    *But for herself she'd not think twice*
*To journey to the seat of war*
    *And help to cook the soldiers' rice.*

*The night wore on and stopped her talk;*
    *Then sobs upon my hearing fell. . . .*
*At dawn when I set forth to walk,*
    *Only the goodman cried farewell!*
                        GILES' version

## DREAMING IN DAYTIME

*My sleeping in broad daylight is not solely because of the shortness of
   the night:*
*There is something in the air of March that makes one drowsy and
   dozy.*
*How the warm breath of the peach-blossoms intoxicates my eye!*
*The sun has set but my dreams are rising still.*
*I dream of my native town, now overgrown with thistles and thorns.*
*I dream of His Majesty and his entourage, so near the beasts of prey.*
*When will the war cease and farmers return to their fields?*
*And when will the petty officials cease to fleece the poor?*

*    *    *    *    *

*How heartless are the overfed ones!*
*Cannibals they are, the eaters of choice foods!*
*In the rich families' kitchens meats stink;*
*On the battlefield there are white bones!*

*    *    *    *    *

*Behind the red-painted doors, wine turns sour, and meat stinks:*
*On the roads lie corpses of people frozen to death.*
*A hair-breadth divides opulence and dire penury!*
*This strange contrast fills me with unutterable anguish!*

The last quoted stanza is, perhaps, the most widely known of all his lines, I have heard it recited even by politicians who are otherwise not interested in poetry. There is no question that these four lines are beautiful. But the question is, where does the beauty lie? Does it lie in the soured wine and stinking meat? Not for me! Does it lie in the frozen bodies on the roads? No! Does it then lie in the contrast? No, I should rather think that it makes the whole phenomenon all the more emphatically ugly. To my mind, the beauty lies in the fact that the strange contrast calls forth such unutterable anguish. In other words, a glaring injustice is exposed and denounced in adequate terms. When injustice is denounced, the negation is negated, and behold! there appears justice in its full effulgence.

I have always thought that justice is beauty as applied to human relations. When we see an innocent person acquitted, we exclaim, "What a fair judgment!" All fair dealings between man and man are beautiful, and all unfair dealings are ugly. And any writings that are strong enough to evoke the sense of justice dormant in our minds are beautiful. I confess I am thoroughly enthralled by the beauty of these lines in St. Mary's Song of Joy:

> *He hath showed strength with his arm;*
> *He hath shattered the proud in the imagination of their heart.*
> *He hath put down princes from their thrones,*
> *And hath exalted them of low degree.*
> *The hungry He hath filled with good things;*
> *And the rich He hath sent empty away.*

I also find superb beauty in these words of St. John: "Flourish, therefore, that ye may fade; be rich for the time, that ye may be beggars for ever.... For it is out of reason that for one belly there should be laid up so much food as would suffice a thousand, and for one body so many garments as would furnish clothing for a thousand men. . . . But wretched and unhappy is the man who would have something more than sufficeth him: for of this come heats of fevers, rigours of cold, diverse pains in all the members of the body, and he can neither be fed nor sated with drink; that covetousness may learn that money will not profit it, which being laid up bringeth to the keepers there of anxiety by day and night, and suffereth them not even for an hour to be quiet and secure" (from *The Apocryphal New Testament*).

It is said that Tu Fu used to boast, in a good-humored way, that his poetry could cure malaria. I don't know about that. But it does serve to vent our pent up feelings against the violent contrast between "heats of fevers" and "rigours of cold" in human society. What "rigours of cold" he himself suffered is vividly described in the following song:

> *It is the eighth moon, when the Autumn skies are high, the wind howls*
> *   angrily.*
> *It sweeps away three layers of grass-roof on my house.*
> *The thatch flies in scattered bits until the shores of the river are strewn*
> *   with them.*
> *Some of them fly high and hang themselves on the tops of tall trees.*
> *The low-flying ones whirl down into the hollows of the marsh.*
>
> *A swarm of small boys from the South Village, taking advantage of my*
> *   feeble age,*
> *Seize the bits under my very nose and run into the bamboo groves.*

*I shout at them until my lips are scorched and throat dry, but they turn*
    *a deaf ear to me.*
*I return home, leaning on my staff, sighing and musing on my fate.*

*After awhile, the wind stops, but the clouds become inkish,*
*Until the Autumn skies are blackened all over and hang above our heads*
    *like a brooding gloom.*
*Our cloth blankets, worn out and stiffened, are as cold as iron.*
*My spoiled kid, whose bed manners are bad, kicks hard at the blanket*
    *until his toes peep out from the holes.*
*Under the leaking roof, there is not a single dry spot in our beds.*
*The rain, as thick-set as hemp, never ceases to pour.*

*Ever since the rebellion and disorder, I have never been able to sleep*
    *well;*
*And tonight, with my body soaked all over, how could I enjoy a*
    *single wink?*

*Ah for a big mansion of a thousand, or ten thousand rooms*
*To give shelter and cheer to all the poor scholars of the world!*
*Safe from the ravages of wind and rain, they will feel as calm as a*
    *mountain.*
*Ah me! The day on which I shall see such a mansion rise before my*
    *eyes,*
*I shall be happy to live in a broken hut by myself and be frozen to*
    *death all alone.*

But of all Tu Fu's "social poems," I like this one best:

## A BRIDE'S FAREWELL TO HER GROOM

*A vine should intertwine itself with an evergreen.*
*Entangled with the weeds, how could it creep high?*
*To marry a girl to a soldier*
*Is to cast her away by the side of a road.*

*Only yesterday were our hairs knotted together.*
*Hardly has our nuptial bed been warmed.*
*This morning you will take leave of me;*
*Is it not a bit too soon?*

*Although your destination is not far,*
*As you are going to stand guard on this side of the river,*
*Yet my humble body being still a virgin's,*
*How can I serve your mother as my mother-in-law?*

*When my parents brought me up,*
*They kept me day and night in the house.*
*But a girl must have someone to cling to,—*
*Even a cock or a dog is better than none.*

*Now you are going to live in the neighborhood of death!*
*I feel my heart has sunk under the weight of intense pain.*
*How I wish to go with you!*
*But what's the use of wishing the impossible?*

*Don't let any thought of me distract you*
*From your heavy duties among the ranks!*
*The presence of a woman in the camp*
*Would wreck the morale of the soldiers.*

*Ah me! A daughter of a poor family,*
*It took me long to acquire these clothes of gauze and silk.*
*I shall no longer wear them in your absence.*
*Even before you go, let me wash away the powder and rouge from my*
    *face.*

*Behold the birds flying in the sky!*
*Big and small, they all soar in pairs.*
*Only the human world goes awry,*
*Rending apart what love has joined together!*

    This poem is, in its original language, so beautiful and full of en-
chanting music that I cannot help wishing that I had the pen of Shakespeare to do it full justice in English. As it is, a great part of its fragrance
has evaporated in the process of translation. But I hope the reader will
get something of the tender sentiments with which the poem is saturated. And I wish also to point out at this juncture some of the similari-
ties that seem to me to exist between Tu Fu and Shakespeare. (I had
called Shakespeare a Spring bird; now I am convinced he belongs to
Summer.) In the first place, both of them seem to possess the happy
knack of entering into the soul of another person and identifying themselves with him. Secondly, like Shakespeare, Tu Fu could introduce
comedy into a tragical situation, and mingle the real and commonplace
with poetry. Thirdly, both seem to believe in a moral order in the universe to which the human world must try to conform if it doesn't want
to go awry. They hold their mirrors up to Nature not only in the sense
that their descriptions are lifelike, but also in the more important sense

that they measure things human by the standard of a higher law. Finally, the singer-saint of China seems to share with the singer-saint of England a heart on fire with love—"a heart burning with compassion for every phase of human misery, physical or moral, and wonderful in its sympathy with the lowly and the poor." (These words I have taken from a truly remarkable book, *Saint Therese of Lisieux; The Little Flower of Jesus*.) As a result of these qualities which they have in common, they are at once fiery and watery. As Tu Fu would put it,

> *A hidden fire is constantly cooking a jade spring,*
> *Which bubbles forth its waters to swell a quiet crevice.*

Is it not remarkable that in his last sonnet Shakespeare should have used exactly the same image? There he spoke of "a cool well,"

> *Which from love's fire took heat perpetual,*
> *Growing a bath and healthful remedy*
> *For men diseas'd.*

And he concluded with a line which fits Tu Fu as well as himself:

> *Love's fire heats water, water cools not love.*

Other poets, so far as I know, have either more fire than water or more water than fire. Dante belongs to the former, while Goethe belongs to the latter. But in Tu Fu and Shakespeare they have attained a perfect balance. I hope the reader will see my point as we go along.

While Tu Fu was opposed point-blank to all wars of aggression and self-aggrandizement, he was too much of a patriot to bear with equanimity the invasions of his country by other peoples. I wonder if any human being could feel more happy than he did when he heard that some lost territories had been retaken by the royal troops from the rebels:

> *Happy news has just reached this remote part of the world!*
> *The royal troops have re-taken the territories along the Yellow River!*
> *I was so overjoyed on hearing it that warm tears gushed from my eyes,*
> *Until my clothes were drenched all over.*
> *All traces of sadness have left the faces of my wife and children.*
> *I pack up my books hurriedly, and I am maddened by joy.*
> *I sing loudly in the broad daylight and abandon myself to wine.*
> *Isn't it heavenly to return to our village in the company of green Spring?*

The happiness that Tu Fu felt when he wrote the poem was more than the silvery gladness of Spring. It was much warmer and denser. There is something aestival about it. It reminds me of the first of the thirty-three moments of happiness that Chin Shengt'an knew in his life:

> *It is a hot day in June when the sun hangs still in the sky and there is not a whiff of wind or air, nor a trace of clouds; the front and back yards are hot like an oven and not a single bird dares to fly about. Perspiration flows down my whole body in little rivulets. There is the noon-day meal before me, but I cannot take it for the sheer heat. I ask for a mat to spread on the ground and lie down, but the mat is wet with moisture and flies swarm about to rest on my nose and refuse to be driven away. Just at this moment when I am completely helpless, suddenly there is a rumbling of thunder and big sheets of black clouds over-cast the sky and come majestically on like a great army advancing to battle. Rain water begins to pour down from the eaves like a cataract. The perspiration stops. The clamminess of the ground is gone. All flies disappear to hide themselves and I can eat my rice. Ah, is this not happiness?*
>
> From LIN YUTANG's *The Importance of Living*

But even in prosecuting a war of defence, Tu Fu held that it would be utterly unpardonable to kill more men than absolutely necessary. This is the burden of the following song:

> *Bows should be drawn with a firm hand and strong,*
> *And the arrows you use should be sharp and long.*
> *In shooting men, shoot first the horses they ride;*
> *In taking prisoners, first capture the Wang.*
> *In killing men, be sure to keep within the limits of necessity!*
> *In defending a nation, to go beyond your borders would be wrong*
> *For the object is to ward off aggression and invasion,*
> *And not to indulge in massacres and devastation!*

What a noble voice we are hearing here! And what an interfusion of strength and tendeness! The refined aesthetes may object to this kind of poem as a bit of moralizing, but what do they know about beauty? Beauty is like happiness in that when it comes at all, it comes like a thief. But if you make it the object of pursuit, it runs away from you like a shy maiden. To my mind, nothing can be more beautiful than flashes of moral insight coming directly and spontaneously from the heart. To go a step farther, I would say all genuine beauty is a by-product of bringing our souls nearer to God; and the reason why war is so ugly is because it makes the earth, which ought to be the play-ground of the children of God, so much like Hell.

But Tu Fu assures us:

> *The butchers of men in this world*
> *Will soon receive the wages of their sin.*

One great quality of Tu Fu is that while he would never bow to the powerful and haughty, he never kicked anybody who was already down. For instance, we have seen how critical he was of Ming Huang in the heyday of his glory, and about Yang Kuei-fei and her sisters and their cousin Yang Kuo-chung, the rotten prime minister, he could write such satirical lines as:

> *Full of coquettish charms and high-flown notions,—*
> *Ah! What veritable embodiments of chastity and virture!*
> *      *      *      *      *
> *The yang flowers fall like snowflakes,*
> *And mingle with the white frogbit.*
> *The blue bird flies away,*
> *Holding a rose-red handkerchief in its beak.*

This is Tu Fu's symbolic way of describing the widely rumored promiscuous union between Yang Kuo-chung and one of the Yang sisters. He compares the latter to the yang flowers (Chinese name for the willow catkins), and Kuo-chung to the frogbit. That they are both white in color symbolizes their coming from the same family. As to the "blue bird," an old commentator, Ho Yi-meng, subtly hinted that it reminded him of these lines from *The Book of Songs*:

> *Heigh, be quiet, be gentle.*
> *Heigh, touch not my handkerchief.*
> *Take care, or the dog will bark.*

The only difference is that in the present case, the handkerchief was touched, and the dog, the faithful watchdog of the common decencies of life, did bark, and how musically he barked! But the point is that the poem was written when the Yang family was actually the power behind the throne, when as Tu Fu put it:

> *Their light dazzles one's eyes, their heat scorches one's hands,*
> *Their power and influence, how extraordinary!*

*Take care! Don't come near them!*
*Are you not afraid of the prime minister's ire?*

One feels that there must be something in the atmosphere that caused our poet to sneeze so loudly. But such extraordinary influence could never last long, for as P. G. Wodehouse put it, "it's always just when a chappie is feeling particularly top-hole, and more than usually braced with things in general that fate sneaks up behind him with a bit of lead piping." And sure enough, the lead piping did come. For soon afterwards, An Lu-shan rebelled, and the emperor had to escape to Szechuen, and Yang Kuei-fei was executed on the way. Our poet himself was hiding somewhere in the capital (Ch'angan) which had fallen to the rebels. It was then that he wrote "A Lamentation" in which, as the reader will see, he no longer carps upon the faults of Ming Huang and Kuei-fei, but simply bewails their fate. The very fire of love that he bore in his belly which had flared forth into furious flames when he saw the empire being misdirected and heading toward a catastrophe melted him into tears when he saw how the culpables suffered from their own failings. There is a Chinese proverb that you must not throw a stone at somebody down in a well, and Tu Fu would not be a worthy representative of our people if he did. Moreover, when one sees before one's very eyes a concrete illustration of the terrible truth that the mills of God grind slowly, yet they grind exceeding small, one is awestruck and has no time to celebrate the downfall of even one's enemies. After all, with all his failings, Ming Huang was one of the most lovable monarchs in the history of China.

## A LAMENTATION

*A wild old man from Shao Ling, I weep silently, gulping down my tears,*
*As I saunter stealthily along the meandering banks of the Ch'u River.*
*The Spring is in its full splendor, but the palaces and temples are all*
*   bolted—*
*For whom then do the tender willows and new iris don their lovely green?*
*I remember, in the old days, when the rainbow-banners fluttered in the*
*   South Park,*
*Everything basking in the sun of royal favor brightened up its*
*   countenance.*
*The first lady of the Chao Yang Court,*
*She used to sit in the royal chariot by the side of the monarch.*

*Before the chariot a group of pretty courtiers rode forth with bows and
  arrows in their hands,
Their white horses champing proudly at their gold bits.
Bending back agilely, with their faces to the sky, they shot into the
  clouds;
With a smile they brought down a pair of winged creatures.
Now where is the lady with such bright eyes and pearly teeth?
The poor wandering soul, defiled by blood, she is doomed to remain
  homeless forever!
The clear Wei River flowing eternally toward the east, the road through
  the Sword Tower penetrating deep into the west,
The dead remained behind, the living journeyed on, between them an
  ever widening gulf!
What man with a heart can help wetting his breast with tears?
O grass and flowers, when will you cease to grow on the shores of this
  river?
At dusk, the Hu cavalry filled the city with dust.
I have to return to the southern suburb, but I gaze far into the north.*

It was Su Tung-p'o who said, "Among all the poets ancient and
modern, Tu Fu holds the superlative place. Is it not because, although a
castaway for life and steeped in hunger and cold, he never took a single
meal without thinking of his sovereign?" I agree, of course, that Tu Fu
is the greatest poet of China. No critic worthy of his salt has ever
doubted it. But I think the reason that Su gave is wide of the mark. Tu
himself had said:

*I remonstrated so fearlessly before the court,
Because I wanted to requite my Creator.*

So, even in court he was thinking more of the Creator than of the
emperor, and it was because he always wanted to requite the love of
the Creator that he loved all His creatures. Among the latter he loved
the common people above all; and he loved his sovereign only as a
potential ally of God:

*I have heard the wise sovereigns of old
Governed their states by lenient laws.
They melted weapons of war into hoes and ploughs.
Indeed, this is the sure way to peace and tranquillity.*

\*  \*  \*  \*  \*

*A common scholar from Tu Lin,*
*My stupidity has grown with age.*
*Sorrowing for the people throughout the seasons,*
*My bosom is burning and sighing like a furnace.*
*Not that the rivers and seas hold no attraction for me,*
*Not that I don't know how to enjoy myself and play with the sun and*
 *the moon:*
*But that being born in the reign of a sage emperor,*
*I was loathe to leave him for good so soon!*

Like all Chinese scholars of lofty ideals, Tu Fu's ambition was above all to be a great statesman, a practical benefactor of the people. He saw that the root of all troubles in human society was the divorce of goodness and power. He said so frankly,

*I want to turn His Majesty into a greater man than Yao and Shun!*

But God had other plans. He wanted to turn Tu Fu into the greatest poet of China, and make him the throat and tongue of the poor. He paved his ways with thorns in order that he might feel the more intimately and keenly the sufferings of others in the same boat. I know of no other poet who suffered so much as he did.

*To dull the edge of hunger I have often lain in bed ten days at a*
 *stretch;*
*My ragged clothes are patched up and knit over more than a hundred*
 *times.*
*You don't see, when twilight drenches these empty walls,*
*How I weep silent tears of blood—silent tears of blood!*

These silent tears of blood quickened his eyes to such an extent that he could see things which would not be observed by the happier ones, who do not see because they do not feel. For instance, he found a hungry eagle pecking at mud, he found a throng of crows pecking at the ulcers of an ownerless lean horse, he found in a recruiting scene that the fat boys had mothers to see them off while the lean ones were standing all alone, he found that the universe was stinking with the blood of men, and he found nothing but tears in the stream of time. To him, history was a brewery of pathos, and he was in such familiar terms with the spirit of history that it became his willing collaborator in the making of his poems. Some of his poems are like window-screens through which the river of time is continually glittering. Far from getting stale, they grow richer in meaning and poignancy with the passing of time. Take this pair of lines:

> *I evoke all the romance of the past,*
> *While I gaze at the city of Kiukiang.*

What a gaze! He poured the whole stream of time into it. In the meantime, twelve centuries have passed since he gazed, and history has brewed more pathos. Indeed, no one knows as well as Tu Fu how to borrow from history. For instance, in one of his quatrains he seems to have caught all that was floating in the air when momentous events were happening. It was a poem to the great court-musician Li Kwei-nien, who had flourished in the heyday of Ming Huang, and whom he met at Kiang-nan fifteen years later. Many things had happened in the interim, and all these events were recalled to life in just four lines:

> *Just at this time, when Spring has reached its meridian,*
> *And flowers are beginning to fall here in Kiang-nan,*
> *I meet you again—you, whose music I used to enjoy years ago*
> *At the houses of the late Prince Chi and Ts'ui Chiu at Ch'ang-an!*

Yes, grief made him see and feel. His sympathies were not confined to the human world. There is, for instance, a touching poem on a sick horse which he had ridden for many years:

> *For a long time I have ridden on you.*
> *How you carried me through the frontier-passes in cold weather!*
> *Your energies have been spent on the dirty roads.*
> *You are old and sick now—what a pain I feel in my heart!*
> *Your mane and bones are not inferior to any of your kind,*
> *Nor have your tameness and decency declined with age.*
> *A humble creature, yes; but who can measure your feelings?*
> *Tender emotions are rising and humming within me.*

There is a cordial warmth in his attitude toward Nature. Like a true democrat, he treats all his fellow-beings as his equals, as members of one big family. Animals, birds, fish, insects, and flowers, all of them seem to confide their secret sorrows to him, because they know that he is their sympathizer and brother in suffering. Does he attribute human feelings to them? No, to him their feeling hearts are palpable realities.

Even the earth has it:

> *Rumbling, rumbling, the thunder is feeling the pulse of the earth.*

And who is more affectionate than the dog:

> *My old dog senses my sorrows,*
> *And stands beside my bed with drooping head.*
>            *       *       *       *       *
> *My old friend the dog, overjoyed at my return,*
> *Whirls around me and disappears into the skirts of my gown.*

Even a little thing like the cricket seems to possess a soul:

### ON THE CRICKET

> *The cricket is a tiny little thing,*
> *And yet how touching are its melancholy notes!*
> *Feeling too chilly to sing under the roots of grass,*
> *It comes indoors to keep you company under the bed.*
> *Its music can melt a lonely traveler into tears,*
> *And make a widow feel as though the dawn would never come.*
> *What silk-strings and bamboo-pipes are half as moving*
> *As this simple music of Nature?*

On a withering orange-tree he observed feelingly:

> *Seared, half-dead leaves*
> *Still cling on to the withered branches:*
> *For it would break their hearts*
> *To bid goodbye to their old homes.*

To him, the hearts of these half-dead leaves have just as much objective reality as his own heart, of which he wrote after an attack of paralysis:

> *My heart is half-dead, with the other half still feeling the wounds of life.*

# SUMMER:
# ITS PLEASANT SHADES

*Fair, kind, and true, have often liv'd alone,*
*Which three till now, never kept seat in one.*
SHAKESPEARE

*When sorrow comes, read Tu Fu and Han Yu,*
*And you will feel as though a fairy hand were scratching at your itch!*
TU MU

*In motion, it was like thunder and lightning boiling with intense anger:*
*At rest, it was like a calm ocean crystallized into serene light.*
TU FU on a Sword Dance.

SO FAR, WE have only seen Summer in its dinner jacket, as it were.
Now we want see it in slippers and dressing gown. Who has not known
some gracious hours of breezy Summer afternoon, when the air is filled
with the warm aroma of roses and the lulling drone of insects, when
the cows drowse lazily in the wide meadows, when Nature itself seems
to unbutton its waistcoat and put its feet up? In fact, Su Shun-ching, a
great poet of the Sung Dynasty, seems to regard this aspect of Summer
as its very essence; for in a poem on "The Idea of Summer," he says

In a secluded summer house, I sleep supinely on a cool mat of fine
  bamboo.
The pomegranate is in full bloom and glitters through the screens.
The ground is full of shades cast by the leafy trees in the noontide sun.
Between my dreams I catch some intermittent notes of the darting
  orioles.

Nobody can appreciate and enjoy such moments of lassitude more than Tu Fu himself:

> *A gentle breeze is blowing, butterflies are frolicking.*
> *Flowers are blazing, and honey bees buzzing,*
> *I sip wine leisurely to enjoy its fine flavors deeply,*
> *I compose a poem and weigh its merits on the delicate scales of my mind.*

And nobody can know more intimately the diligent indolence of a Summer day:

### HOME JOYS

> *My home is girdled by a limpid stream,*
>> *And there in summer days life's movements pause,*
> *Save where some swallow flits from beam to beam,*
>> *And the wild sea-gull near and nearer draws.*
> *The good wife rules a paper board for chess;*
>> *The children beat a fish-hook out of wire;*
> *My ailments call for physic more or less,*
>> *What else should this poor frame of mine require?*
>>> GILES' version

If we remember that there were days in Summer when Tu Fu was simply maddened by the heat and felt like uttering a loud cry, we cannot help wondering what various qualities are contained in Summer's bosom. The same holds for the poetry of Tu Fu. We have already heard some of his loud cries. Now we shall address ourselves to those charming poems which he hit off in a light mood, when he took life easy and his high-strung nerves had lapsed into a sort of sweet torpor. For Tu Fu is not only a nightingale who sings so loud that the hawthorn seems too frail for the vigor of his song, but also a blackbird whose whistle, as Richard Jefferies knew so well, is very human, like someone playing the flute, who strives to express his keen appreciation of the loveliness of the days, the golden glory of the meadow, the light, and the luxurious shadows.

First let us take up some of his delectable Nature poems, which present a veritable riot of roses. We have to content ourselves with a few specimens here:

## BEAUTIES OF NATURE

Sprinkling a footpath, aspen flowers spread a white carpet.
Floating on a brooklet, the lotus-leaves overlap like green coins.
Amidst bamboo-shoots baby-pheasants lie hidden from the human eye.
On the sand young wild ducks nestle quietly 'neath their mothers'
    wings.

## A COMPLAINT TO SPRING

The sorrows of an exile fill my eyes and inebriate my heart.
The vagabond Spring Genie has arrived around the river-bower.
He sends all the buds into flowering—rash enough on his part!
And what is more, he teaches the nightingales to sing with such
    persistent power!

## THE THIEVERY OF THE SPRING WIND

The peaches and pears planted with my own hands are not without
    owner.
My walls are low, 'tis true, but they enclose a humble home.
The east wind apparently took me for a fool!
Like a burglar in the night he broke down some sprays of my flowers!

## THE LAVISH HOSPITALITY OF SPRING

    The river deep, the bamboos quiet,
    Only a couple of homes around here.
    The fussy flowers, red and white,
    Vie with one another in beauty and charm.
    Now I have found the place to requite
    The lavish hospitality of Spring!
    All that I need is sweet wine
    To sweeten the rest of my days.

## MADAM HUANG'S GARDEN

    Rows upon rows of flowers
    In the little garden of Madam Huang!
    All the branches are heavy-laden
    With countless clusters of flowers.

*The carefree butterflies loiter around them,*
*And start dancing from time to time.*
*The lovely orioles are intoxicated with freedom.*
*"Cheerio, cheerio!" they sing.*

## THE RIOT OF FLOWERS

*The endless flowers on the river bank,*
*How they crash the gates of my eyes and irritate my soul!*
*I have no place to complain of their nuisance,*
*I am simply maddened by their colors.*
*I called on my southern neighbor,*
*Who, like myself, has a great liking for wine.*
*For ten days I have drunk with him,*
*Leaving an empty bed at home!*

## AN INVITATION TO THE HERONS

*The herons used to come to the front of our door,*
*But for reasons unknown to me they have ceased to visit us.*
*Today I chanced upon them on the sandy beach.*
*They looked at me with suspicious eyes.*
*From now on they should know I have nothing in my sleeves,*
*And come as many times as they wish in the course of a day.*

## THE SWALLOW?

*My thatched studio is small and low,*
*And yet the swallows have taken a fancy to it.*
*See, my little friends, how you have soiled my harp and books!*
*Hey! Don't drive the insects to slap my face!*

## TAKE IT EASY!

*From the court every eve to the pawnshop I pass,*
*    To come back from the river the drunkest of men;*
*As often as not I'm in debt for my glass;—*
*    Well, few of us live to be three score and ten.*
*The butterfly flutters from flower to flower,*
*    The dragonfly sips and springs lightly away,*
*Each creature is merry in its brief little hour,*
*    So let us enjoy our short life while we may.*
                                    GILES' *version*

## SOME SELECTED LINES AND STANZAS

*A quiet temple thick-set with flowers;*
*A sequestered lake hidden in the fine bamboos.*
*Oh where come the passionate songs of the nightingale?*
*All alone he has been singing his heart out for hours.*
*   *   *   *   *

*What a lovely patch of green!*
*I know it's grass on the other side of the lake.*
*What a glorious stretch of crimson!*
*I see it's the clouds beyond the eastern sea.*
*   *   *   *   *

*Patches of green have whirled away from us:*
*We have just passed by some lovely ridges.*
*Look! There is something yellow in front of us!*
*I see the orange trees are coming toward us.*
*Things Seen on a Boat Trip*
*   *   *   *   *

*A cluster of red spottings—*
*The flowers in the corner of the house!*
*A patch of green loveliness—*
*The grass by the side of the wall!*
*   *   *   *   *

*A tortoise leaves a watery path behind it,*
*As it sails slowly through the duckweeds.*
*   *   *   *   *

*Kingfishers are chirping on a clothes-line.*
*A dragonfly rests motionless on the silken cord of a fishing rod.*
*   *   *   *   *

*Entering into the peach blossoms,*
*Redness grows soft and tender.*
*Returning to the willow leaves,*
*Greenness becomes fresh and new.*
*   *   *   *   *

*The water being calm, the shadow of the tower stands motionless.*
*   *   *   *   *

*The dark ravine oozes with the music of silence.*
*The bright moonlight is being sifted through the thick foliage.*
*   *   *   *   *

*Ting, ting goes the woodman's axe,*
*And the mountain becomes the more solitary and silent for the sound.*

*    *    *    *    *

*A tiny rivulet trickles like a hidden thread through a flower-path.*
*Spring stars girdle my grass hut like a necklace of pearls.*

*    *    *    *    *

*The emeraldine fine bamboos, in the gentle caress of the wind,*
*Are as coy and quiet as a little maiden.*
*The red water-lilies, bathed in the rain,*
*Send forth whiffs after whiffs of invisible incense.*

*    *    *    *    *

*A petal falls! The oriole chases after it,*
*Taking it for a butterfly.*
*What is that noise on the brooklet?*
*Oh I see, a mink has caught a poor fish!*

*    *    *    *    *

*Countless dragonflies are darting up and down in a group.*
*A pair of wild ducks float and dive together.*

*    *    *    *    *

*White sandy beaches and emerald bamboos*
*Embrace the river village in eventide.*
*The wooden door of my humble house*
*Seems to hold a hearty tete-a-tete with the new moon.*

*    *    *    *    *

*The Autumn water is clear and fathomless.*
*It cleanses and refreshes the heart of a lonely traveler.*

*    *    *    *    *

*The nice rain knows its season,*
*It is born of Spring.*
*It follows the wind secretly into the night,*
*And showers its blessings, silently and softly, upon everything.*

*    *    *    *    *

*The peach-blossoms and the pear-blossoms*
*Follow closely upon one another's heels to the ground.*
*The yellow birds and the white birds*
*Sometimes mingle together in their flight.*

*    *    *    *    *

*The birds are the whiter for the blue of the river;*
*The flowers almost burn on the green hills.*

*    *    *    *    *

*A lamp glimmers upon my sleeplessness.*
*Inwardly calm, I begin to smell the ethereal scent of incense.*

*In the depth of the night the temple strikes me with a sudden awe.*
*The tinkling of the golden bells by the wind brings silence to the fore.*
*Blackness has enveloped the courtyard with all its Spring colors.*
*Dark fragrance is haunting this stainless spot on earth.*

\* \* \* \* \*

*Darting upward, a bee gets entangled in a falling catkin.*
*Forming a queue, the ants are crawling up to a withered pear.*

\* \* \* \* \*

*I seem to see lightness itself!*
*Some stray feathers are sailing before the wind.*
*Recovering from a state of self-forgetfulness,*
*I have caught myself counting the stamens of a flower!*

\* \* \* \* \*

*A-boating in a Spring river, I fell into a trance,*
*And felt as though I were sitting in Heaven!*
*Looking at the flowers through my old eyes,*
*I thought the air must have been very foggy!*

\* \* \* \* \*

*A gentle shower, and the little fish come to the surface;*
*A little breeze, and the swallows are darting with slanting wings.*

\* \* \* \* \*

*The bees and butterflies are all instinct with life;*
*A beautiful dragonfly looks stealthily at a passing shrike.*

\* \* \* \* \*

*The maples and orange trees are playing for us a wonderful orchestra*
   *of colors!*

\* \* \* \* \*

*The evening sun is smoking the fine grass.*
*The luminous river is sparkling through the screen.*

\* \* \* \* \*

*But for the moon hanging above the green cliff,*
*Sorrow would have killed a white-headed man!*

\* \* \* \* \*

*I get up late and everything is quiet at home.*
*Indolence makes the place doubly cosy.*

\* \* \* \* \*

*The waters being deep, the fish are extremely happy.*
*The forest being thick, the birds feel quite at home.*

\* \* \* \* \*

*Unable to move about freely,*
*I looked up at the feathered ones shame-facedly.*

\* \* \* \* \*

Before we proceed further with our promenade in the garden of Tu Fu, let us pause awhile to examine the little posy of flowers we have already gathered together, and, if possible, to count their stamens and pistils just for the sheer pleasure of it. To drop metaphor and to speak plainly, what are some of the qualities that have revealed themselves to us in reading over the above specimens? I wish I could have a hearty tete-a-tete with the reader over a glass of beer, and sort out patiently between us one quality after another until everything is straightened out. But as this is impossible in the nature of things, I have to play solitaire. The first thing that impresses me is the remarkable power of observation with which our poet seems to be endowed. His mind is microscopic in intensity. It seems nothing is too small for it to record graphically. I am reminded of some of our artists, now too few, who could carve a wonderful landscape upon the very tiny kernel of a fruit. Among poets, John Keats seems to possess the same quality to similar degree. I can never forget the thrill that went through my mind when, reading his "Endymion," I came upon such a passage as this:

> *Hereat the youth*
> *Look'd up: a conflicting of shame and ruth*
> *Was in his plaited brow: yet, his eyelids*
> *Widened a little, as when Zephyr bids*
> *A little breeze to creep between the fans*
> *Of careless butterflies.*

Another noteworthy thing about Tu Fu is that he is a past master of the chiaroscuro, who likes to put things in black and white. He sees contrasts in colors, and in other things for that matter. The white birds look whiter against the background of the blue waters, and the red flowers seems to pop out from the green hills and burn like candles. He pits a white-headed man against a green cliff, a grass hut against a necklace of stars, a grey wooden door against the new moon, maples against orange trees, and so on. I have found him using the same trick a thousand times, and every time he seems to attain the effect he wants. For instance, in a poem on the great general Li Kwang-pi, we find a most touching line:

*His head white, his heart as red as ever.*

Here again the effect is enhanced by means of a deliberate contrast. As a matter of fact, he makes no secret of his deliberate and patient labor. He confesses it:

> *If my words fail to thrill and please,*
> *I should not die in peace!*

It seems to me what he says of the silk-maid is equally true of himself:

> *With a loving solicitude, a pretty girl*
> *Has ironed the silk till it's perfectly smooth;*
> *And made it into a nice cloth,*
> *Which appears a seamless whole.*

Perhaps it may be said (as Dr. Sun Fo once pointed out to me a few years ago) that his discriptions of Nature are not so spontaneous as those of Wang Wei and Li Po, but what he loses in spontaneity he gains in emphasis. And we should remember that they belong to different seasons, and Summer cannot reproduce the virginal freshness of Spring, any more than Spring could have attained to the wide awareness, incisive clarity and white-hot concentration of Summer. The other day I ran across in James Joyce's *Ulysses* a quaint expression: Poetical idea pink, then golden, then grey, then black. Still true to life also. I find it somewhat true also of the Poetry of T'ang. For while the Spring poets were pink, Tu Fu is golden, and there can be no reversal of the seasons. As to whether Autumn and Winter will be grey and black, we shall see later.

But what makes this little posy of flowers and petals especially lovely is the sweet perfume of sympathy emanating constantly from them.

> *The rose looks fair, but fairer we it deem,*
> *For that sweet odour which doth in it live.*

For our poet has a genuine love for the little things in Nature. When the herons ceased to come to him, he really missed them. When he saw the birds moving freely about among the woods, he really felt a sense of shame within him, because he had lost his freedom at that time. On the other hand, when he called the flowers "a nuisance" and the Spring

genie "a vagabond," and complained about the swallows soiling his
harp and books and driving the insects to slap his face, he really loved
them so much that he wanted to hide it, just as a fond mother would
say to her guests what a naughty boy her little Johnnie is. Once he
invited some friends to his house, and complained to them about the
deafening noise made by the cicadas:

> *Who says my home is quiet?*
> *Listen, what a row the cicada makes!*

Maybe, that time he was truly annoyed, but who can blame him for
that little aberration from his usual good humor, seeing that no less
a lover of the cicada than J. H. Fabre has felt the same:

*Ah! Creature possessed, the plague of my dwelling, which I hoped would be so
peaceful!—the Athenians, they say, used to hang you up in a little cage, the better
to enjoy your song. One were well enough, during the drowsiness of digestion; but
hundreds, roaring all at once, assaulting the hearing until thought recoils—this
indeed is torture! You put forward, as excuse, your rights as the first occupant.
Before my arrival the two plane-trees were yours without reserve; it is I who have
intruded, have thrust myself into their shade. I confess it; yet muffle your cymbals,
moderate your arpeggio, for the sake of your historian!*

At any rate, Tu Fu is one of the most humorous poets I have ever read.
It would seem that his dire poverty made him extremely rich in humor. Here are some lines from "The Song of An Empty Pouch":

> *Let others take part in the mad hunt for riches;*
> *My way leads through difficulties and straits!*
> \* \* \* \* \*
> *To spare my pouch the shame of complete emptiness,*
> *I leave my last cash in it to keep it company.*

On another occasion, he sang about a fish-shaped pouch of red silk,
given to him by the emperor as a kind of badge:

> *I am still wearing the fish-shaped pouch,*
> *Awarded to me by his majesty.*
> *What if I am old and poor!*
> *The pouch contains at least an echo!*

The jolly old man not only derived much fun from poverty, but also enjoyed other misfortunes of life, such as having his hat blown off by the wind:

> What a shame! The wind blew off my hat,
> Exposing to the full light a bald head!
> I had a good laugh and requested a bystander
> To put the hat on my head with special care.

Even more serious misfortunes than this did not dampen his good spirits. When he became deaf he sang:

> Deaf have my ears been since last month.
> My eyes—ah, when will they be blind?
> Monkey howlings no autumn tears will call forth from me.
> Nor will the noisy chirps of sparrows breed my evening sorrows.
> Just now I saw yellow leaves fall from the mountain trees,
> And I asked my son, "The wind is roaring, isn't it?"
> WEN YUAN-NING'S version

Here is another delightful piece of self-mockery:

> With my face turned upward, I gazed and gazed at the birds.
> When I heard someone call somebody else, I answered, "Yes, I am coming!"
> In reading books I skip over difficult words.
> In drinking wine one bottle is not enough.

This kind of humor, that is, making jokes at the expense of oneself, is what I should like to call a typically Chinese humor. Su Tung-p'o seems to be a worthy follower of Tu Fu, since he too could make fun of himself:

> I am an old man, and yet I wear a flower in my hair!
> I am not ashamed, because I have a thick-skinned face!
> But I see the flower is blushing on my head,
> To find itself in such an unfitting place!
> I am drunk, and need someone to lean upon as I walk home;
> It will give the pedestrians a pleasant surprise.
> At least half of the window-curtains will be lifted up,
> And pretty girls will peep at me with admiring eyes!

The reason why this type of humor is particularly valuable to us is because it is a corrective to our excessive fear of losing face. When we are poor, we pretend to be rich. When we are bald-headed, we pretend to be as hairy as a Pekinese. When we are deaf, we pretend to hear. When we are fools, we pretend to know a great deal by keeping a sage-like silence. And even when we are dead, we pretend to be very much alive by making our funeral procession as pompous an affair as a military parade. When we are humbugs, we pretend to be big bugs. In one word, we are afraid to be laughed at, or looked down upon. When, therefore, we see real big bugs like Tu Fu and Su Tung-p'o enjoying such a good laugh over their own follies, we feel that after all our face is not such a precious thing. I would call the Tu Fu-like humor our national humor, precisely because it helps to expose the most prevailing humbug among us. For if we want to save our soul, we must first be prepared to lose our face.

But the question is, where did Tu Fu get all his humor? My answer is that it was partly due to natural endowment, but mostly due to suffering. For one thing, suffering makes the prospect of life brighter by lessening the fear of death. The evanescence of life which to the happy ones is such a tragic idea is a source of happiness to the sufferer. As Tu Fu says:

> My path is paved with thorns all through.
> Thank God, my days are numbered too!

This is exactly what St. Therese of Lisieux says in a letter to her sister: "Thought of the shortness of life gives me courage, and helps me to put up with the weariness of the journey. What matters a little toil upon earth?" For another thing, anyone who has experienced great sorrows and emerged from them without a nervous breakdown will be able to stand the little annoyances of life and even regard them as sweetmeats. But before I ride my hobby horse of philosophizing, let us first listen to his own story:

> After a whole year's journey, I arrived at my thatched hut,
> And found my wife in rags and tatters.
> Deeply touched, our loud cries were echoed by the sighing pines,
> And our stifled sobs blended with the sad music of the flowing brook.
> My little son whom I used to fondle so much looked paler than the snow.
> Seeing his father, he turned away his face and wept silently.
> Dirty and greasy, he wore no socks on his feet.
> In front of the bed stood my two little girls, with their seamy dresses

*barely covering their knees:*
*I saw the embroidered sea-waves were all broken and disconnected,*
*And the purple phoenixes and water-sprits dismembered beyond*
*    recognition.*
*For several days, preyed upon by depression and illness,*
*I had lain in bed, vomiting and purging.*
*With no money in my purse,*
*How can I save my family from being frozen?*
*But my wife has taken out some old silk quilts,*
*And opened the cosmetics she had laid away during my absence.*
*I see beauty gradually returning to her emaciated face;*
*And the girls, idiotic little things, are combing their own hair.*
*They ape their mother in every way:*
*In their morning coiffeur, they help themselves to the cosmetics:*
*They paint their faces haphazardly with vermillion and white powder,*
*And draw their eyebrows so broad that they look like comic masks*
*Coming back alive, and looking fondly at my kids,*
*I almost forget our dire penury.*
*And what naughty kids they are! They storm me with endless questions*
*    and even pull my beard!*
*But who can be angry with them just now?*
*When I remember how miserable I was in the hands of the brigands,*
*I find it very sweet indeed to be pestered by the noise and clamor*
*    of my little ones.*
*Newly reunited, it is for us to be nice to each other and make the*
*    best of life,*
*Before we think of the problem of livelihood.*

Anybody who has had any dealings at all with children will sym-
pathize with our poet. Even Confucius knew that children were not
easy to handle. "When you treat them too intimately, they would
throw all your dignity to the winds." For instance, they pull your
beard. I am sure Confucius must have had some unpleasant experience
of that sort, before he could utter such a pungent truth. But I am not
thinking so much of the dignity factor as the mental wear-and-tear one
has to undergo in living with lots of children. Just at the time when
you sit down at your desk rolling up your sleeves as if you were going
to produce a real masterpiece, you hear a noise in the next room which
sounds very much like a hurdy-gurdy. Just when you are not in a
talking mood, they pester you with questions, some of which are not

particularly easy to answer. "Daddy, how high is the sky?" Not wanting to show the seamy side of your knowledge, you take down from the shelves such books as Jeans' *The Mysterious Universe*, Eddington's *The Expanding Universe* and even Einstein's *The Theory of Relativity*, and after a few feverish searchings in their pages, you find no answer and try to save your face by corking their mouths with some candies. And what is even worse, when you are in a talking mood and feel like telling them a nice Christmas story, they call you down by "Aw, nuts!" and announce the end of your story even before you have started, and you would be a very lucky man indeed if you happen to grow no beard or mustache, although, it is true, your nose is always there to attract the unwelcome attention of the little fingers. Old Benchley knows very well what a trying thing it is to travel with a kiddie of three. And so did our poet, when he and his family, as refugees of war, had to travel on foot through rough roads and wild mountains:

> My idiotic little girl, feeling the gnawing pangs of hunger, bit at my
>    body;
> She wailed loudly, and I was afraid the tigers and wolves might hear,
> So I held her close to my bosom to stop her crying,
> But she struggled hard and wailed even more furiously than before.

There are innumerable accounts of his travels in his poems, but he has presented them in a nutshell in just two lines:

> For ten years, I have been tossed to and fro like a silken ball,
> And I had to carry my chicks along to the farthest ends of the earth.

All this may sound a little melancholy and not particularly humorous, but Tu Fu could very well answer in the words of Shakespeare, "I have neither the scholar's melancholy, which is emulation; nor the musician's, which is fantastical; nor the courtier's, which is proud; nor the soldier's, which is ambitious; nor the lawyer's, which is politic; nor the lady's, which is nice; nor the lover's, which is all these; but it is the melancholy of mine own, compounded of many simples, extracted from many objects, and indeed, the sundry contemplation of my travels; which, by often rumination, wraps me in a most humorous sadness." But you ask how one could be sad and humorous at the same time. As to this, Tu Fu himself has given us a clue to the answer:

*When I remember how miserable I was in the hands of the brigands, I find it very sweet indeed to be pestered by the noise and clamor of my little ones.*

In suffering he has found the key to happiness. For happiness, like the boiling point, is relative. A given situation in life would pass unnoticed or even prove annoying if worse circumstances had not been experienced. In passing through sad circumstances to better ones, one feels the external pressure lightened, while the mind still retains the power of resistance called forth by the former situation; and there arises the boiling point of happiness. In order to be happy most of your days, you must always remember the blackest days of your life. Otherwise happiness will lead you a wild-goose chase. When a man is on the point of drowning, all he cares for is his life. But as soon as he gets ashore, he asks, "Where is my umbrella?" The wisdom of life consists in not asking for the lost umbrella. And herein lies the secret of Tu Fu's invincible cheerfulness of spirit. But of course, I don't mean to say that it is a very pleasant thing to lose your umbrella. No, it is a sad thing, especially to a poor man. What I mean is that since you are not drowned in water, that sadness at least ought to be drowned in humor, and when this happens you get what Shakespeare calls a humorous sadness.

Li Po was humorsome, because, the poor man, he remembered his happiest days. Tu Fu was humorous, because, the happy man, he remembered his darkest days. The former was like a speculator in Wall Street who bought at the highest quotation and watched the price go down every day until he found himself a bankrupt; but the latter was like one who sold short and watched himself growing richer every day until he became the biggest shareholder in the Bank of Happiness. For the fact is, Li Po regarded himself as an angel exiled, for reasons that mystified him, from Heaven; while Tu Fu regarded himself as a dead man miraculously come back home alive, and finding his wife and his little ones miraculously spared from the ravages of war. Here is another touching poem which the reader cannot afford to miss:

> *The crimson clouds on the west*
> *Spread before me like a gorgeous panorama.*
> *The foot of the sun has just gone down*
> *Below the level of the earth.*
> *On arriving at the door of my thatched hut,*
> *I hear sparrows and other birds sing a chorus.*

*At last, I am at home again*
*After travelling a thousand li.*
*My wife and my children marvel*
*That I am still alive.*
*Recovering from their first shock,*
*They weep and wipe tears from their eyes.*
*The world is still in a broil,*
*And human life is like dust in the wind.*
*Have I really returned alive?*
*How precarious an event it looks!*
*Our neighbors have come in crowds*
*To peer at me over the walls.*
*Moved by sympathy,*
*They sigh and snivel.*
*In the depth of the night.*
*Under a glimmering candlelight,*
*My wife and I sit silently face to face,—*
*It seems as though we had met in a dream.*

And the interesting thing is that he had hardly expected his family to survive the horrible massacres perpetrated around his home of which he had learned. The following poem is too deservedly famous to omit even in such a casual survey as this:

*Last year the T'ung Pass was broken through*
*By the rebel troops.*
*I was separated for a long time*
*From my wife and children.*
*In the summer of this year,*
*When grass and trees were growing thick,*
*I managed to run away from the brigands*
*And came here westward.*
*Wearing hemp shoes,*
*I saw the Son of Heaven;*
*My sleeves were in rags and holes,*
*From which my two elbows peeped at His Majesty!*
*The court was touched by my return alive,*
*And my old friends pitied my ugly features.*
*In tears I accepted the censorship,*
*So grateful I was to the kind Emperor.*
*Though I was homesick,*

*I could not bring myself to broach the subject.*
*I sent a letter to San Ch'uan,*
*To ascertain whether my family was still there.*
*Later I heard that the whole village*
*Fell a prey to the barbarians;*
*Not a single life was spared,*
*Not even the dogs and cocks.*
*After such a wholesale massacre,*
*How can I expect my family to have survived alone?*
*I look at yonder precipitous mountains,*
*The whole earth seems to have become a den of tigers.*
*My sorrows form into a hard knot,*
*Which nobody can untie.*
*Since I sent the letter,*
*Ten months have elapsed.*
*Now I am no longer expecting any news.*
*On the contrary, I sorely fear lest any news should come.*
*I don't know why this sudden change from expectation to fear,—*
*This inch-long heart within me, what a mystery it is!*

So, at the end of our journey, we find ourselves again at the threshold of mystery. Indeed, all roads seem to lead to it, provided they are long enough. We already saw how Li Po soared and soared until a limit was reached:

*Let me lay down my cup for a moment and ask:*
*O Sky! Since how long did you have the moon?*

Now we have watched Tu Fu diving like a bucket in a concealed well and exploring the penetralia of his heart and finally discovering its unfathomableness:

*This inch-long heart within me, what a mystery it is!*

It would seem the universe is a mystery in and out and whether you gauge it horizontally or perpendicularly. Then what have we got from our arduous pilgrimage to the shrine of Tu Fu? Nothing except that he has made us more aware of our ignorance and littleness. As he puts it explicity:

*Saints and sages regard themselves as little or nothing.*

This humility is no false modesty, but is born of a true insight into the mystery of life. As Einstein says, "The most beautiful thing we can experience is the mysterious. It is the source of all true art and science. He to whom this emotion is a stranger, who can no longer pause to wonder and stand rapt in awe is as good as dead: his eyes are closed." And Tu Fu is such a great poet, precisely because he opens our eyes to the mystery that we carry within us, and thus bring us nearer to God who is the source of all mysteries.

# AN INTERLUDE

> Salamander
> *Happy, happy glowing fire!*
> *Zephyr*
> *Fragrant air! delicious delight!*
> *Dusketha*
> *Let me to my glooms retire!*
> *Breama*
> *I to green-weed rivers bright!*
> KEATS, "Song of Four Faeries."

*The tendinous part of the mind, so to speak, is more developed in winter; the fleshy, in summer. I should say winter had given the bone and sinew to literature, summer the tissues and the blood.* JOHN BURROUGHS

> *All sorts of things and weather*
> *Must be taken in together*
> *To make up a year.*
> EMERSON

"SPORADIC GREAT MEN," says William James, "come everywhere. But for a community to get vibrating through and through with intensely active life, many geniuses coming together and in rapid succession are required. This is why great epochs are so rare—why the sudden bloom of a Greece, an early Rome, a Renaissance, is such a mystery. Blow must follow blow so fast that no cooling can occur in the intervals.

Then the mass of the nation grows incandescent, and may continue to glow by pure inertia long after the originators of its internal movement have passed away."

In this James has hit upon the first requisite, the *sine qua non,* of any vital movement in the cultural history of mankind. How well the poetry of T'ang fulfilled this condition can, among other evidence, be substantiated by the fact that around the date of Tu Fu's death there were born no less than three literary lions, each supreme in his own field. Tu Fu passed away in 770. Two years before that date Han Yu had seen the light. Two years after that Po Chü-i came, accompanied by a lesser poet, Liu Yu-shi, who was to be one of his lifelong friends. And then the next year saw the birth of the last of the mighty triumvirate, Liu Chung-yuan.

There are some interesting anecdotes which help us to visualize how popular poetry had come to be in the whole period of T'ang. Once three poets, Wang Tsu-huan, Kao Shih, and Wang Chang-ling were having a *petit souper* together in a wine shop. There came later a group of actors from the Imperial Theatre to attend a banquet being held upstairs. Then a few singsong girls arrived one after another. A brilliant party it was, with music. The three poets, in a *jeu d'esprit,* agree among themselves that they would determine their relative merits by the number of their songs that would be sung by the actors and sing-song girls. By and by they heard an actor sing a song by Wang Chang-ling, which contains these well-known lines:

> *If my friends in Loyang should ask about me,*
> *Tell them that my heart is pure as the ice in a jade cup.*

Thereupon Chang-ling marked it down and said airily, "So friends, I have scored one." Then another actor took up a song by Kao Shih, with these lines:

> *On opening my handbag, tears wetted my breast;*
> *For I saw my sweetheart's letter of the other day.*

With equal elation he marked it down and said, "So I too have scored one." Sometime later, another actor sang, and it was again a poem by Wang Chang-ling. You can imagine how exalted he must have felt, having scored a second time. But think of poor Wang Tsu-huan, who had none whatever to his credit! He certainly was greatly exasperated by the humiliation, but he did not give up hope. "These vulgar things, the actors, what do they know?" he said. "It's in their nature to prefer the familiar to the exquisite. But I am quite confident that when it comes to the turn of the sing-song girls, the most beautiful one will sing one of my songs. I'll stake my life and honor upon it!" Strangely enough, it came off exactly as he had expected. For the most beautiful girl did pick up his song, which has been on the lips of every student of Chinese poetry for more than a millennium:

> The Yellow River climbs up far into the white clouds;
> The Great Wall runs through all the ridges like a continuous thread.
> Why should the western pipe "complain about the willows"?
> The breath of Spring has never passed beyond the Gate of Jade.

What a relief it must have been to Tsu-huan! "You country boys," he said to his friends triumphantly, "did you think I was bragging?"

But, perhaps, no poet in the world, as Arthur Waley has assured us, has ever enjoyed greater contemporary popularity than Po Chü-i. Waley has put it so neatly that I will borrow a passage from him:

His poems were on the mouths of kings, princes, concubines, ladies, plough-boys, and grooms. They were inscribed on the walls of village schools, temples, and ships-cabins. A certain Captain Kao Hsia-yu was courting a dancing-girl. "You must not think I am an ordinary dancing-girl," she said to him, "I can recite Master Po's Everlasting Wrong." And she put up her price.

These anecdotes, which I have selected out of a great number, ought to be sufficient to show how the community in the time of T'ang was actually vibrating through and through with the pulse of poetry. If William James had known Chinese and made a study of T'ang poetry, I am sure he would have mentioned it alongside the other great movements. But what would probably have surprised him most was the strange phenomenon that one group of singers after another came upon the scene and each group sang almost like a prearranged chorus to give full expression to the spirit of the particular season to which it belonged. A great variety of voices participated in each chorus, but together they formed a superb harmony. "Distinct as the billows, yet one as the sea."

I have not followed closely the stages of the other great movements that James mentioned. I am only slightly acquainted with the evolution of Roman Law. It too had four periods, namely, *ius civile, ius gentium, ius naturale,* and finally codification by Justinian. But I hardly can see a succession of seasons in that movement, but only a progressive liberalization. On the other hand, the poetry of T'ang forms such a living year that I cannot explain its stages otherwise than in terms of the seasons. It is really a grand symphony, with its opening, development, change, and conclusion. Integral parts of a whole, they are yet so differentiated from each other that one can without much difficulty tell to what part a particular poem belongs! Reserving my explanation of this wonderful phenomenon to a later stage, I would like to introduce here some concrete illustrations. For example these lines:

> *On the ocean, the sun is born out of the entrails of the night.*
> *Around the river, Spring has overtaken the closing year.*

This makes you feel as though the sun were impatient of the night and wanted to anticipate the dawn, as though Spring were racing like a spirited pony with the New Year and came off with flying colors. I humbly submit that such images would not have occurred, and even if they did, would not have appealed, to any but a poet of the Spring period. And indeed it was written by Wang Wan, an elder contemporary of Li Po. On the other hand, take these lines:

> *I pity the plum-blossoms,*
> *For they are always the flowers of a yester-year!*

The plum-blossoms burst in the twelfth month of the lunar calendar and continue to blow in the New Year. They may very well be regarded as the heralds of Spring, and yet to Li Shang-yin, a typical winter poet, they are always the relics from the last Winter. Don't you see how the poets create Nature in their own image? Tu Fu wrote:

> *A gentle breeze is blowing, butterflies are frolicking.*
> *Flowers are blazing, and honey bees buzzing.*

You feel some cordial warmth in these lines. But you are in an entirely different world when you come across such sentiments as these:

> *All day, I have asked the flowers without getting an answer,*
> *"For whom do you bloom and for whom do you fade?"*
> YEN YÜN

\*    \*    \*    \*    \*

*After you have gathered your honey from all the flowers,*
*What have you got for all your bitter sweetness?*

                                        Lo YIN *on tne bees*

I leave the reader to guess for himself to what season Yen Yün and Lo Yin belong.

Chen Tzu-ang sang hilariously of the Master of Dark Truth, who "was the wide world in a jade cup." But Li Shang-yin feels differently, for, as he says:

*If the wide world is contained in the jade cup,*
*We should still have to wail our separation within the cup!*

Li Po wrote about the waterfall of Lushan:

*Flying straight down three thousand feet,*
*It looks as if the Milky Way had fallen from the sky!*

The same waterfall evokes a different image in the mind of an autumnnal poet, Hsu Ning:

*Eternally wafting like a long sheet of white silk,—*
*A line that divides once for all the mountain into two.*

There is something neat and clear-cut about Autumn. I don't know how a summer poet would describe the same phenomenon, as I have not succeeded in finding an example among the works of Tu Fu and his friends Kao Shih and Tsen Ts'an; but I should imagine they would go for the rough-hewn grandeur of these lines from Keats:

                    *. . . for the solid roar*
*Of thunderous waterfalls and torrents hoarse,*
*Pouring a constant bulk, uncertain where.*

One of the most popular themes with the T'ang poets throughout the seasons is the sorrows of the maids-of-honor waiting in the imperial harem for the uncertain favors of the monarch. A spring poet, Wang Chang-ling, describes their feelings:

*I rose at the peep of dawn, and swept the ground.*
*I have watched the gates of the Gold Temple swing*
    *open one by one.*
*With the moon-like fan in my hand,*

*Let me rest awhile and loiter around.*
*Ah that my fair features should prove no match*
*For the black feathers of you cold raven!*
*See how it brings the sunlight along*
*As it wings its way over the court of Chao Yang!*

This is one of the most famous songs of its genre. How spring-like it is! It is full of longing, and yet full of hope. The sunlight that the cold raven bears on its back symbolizes the coming of the emperor. Now let us listen to Tsen Ts'an, who was six years Tu Fu's junior:

*His Majesty, displeased with my jealous nature,*
*Shut me up in this lonely seraglio.*
*Fresh favors must now be hanging proudly from the dancing sleeves;*
*But the memory of the old love is locked between my knit eyebrows.*
*The green coin-like leaves are growing on the fading footprints before*
  *my door.*
*The rouge on my face melts with my tears and form furrows upon my*
  *cheeks.*
*The peach-blossoms seem to be laughing at me.*
*In sullen silence, I look wistfully at the bright colors of Spring.*

I find something Tu Fu-like about this song. The denseness and poignancy of the feeling, and the vivid contrasts between fresh favors and old love; between sullen silence and bright Spring, are characteristic of Summer. If our first specimen be called a song of innocence, this one may be called a song of experience.

For the period of Autumn, I present two samples, one by Li Yi (circa 770–827), and the other by Po Chü-i, both of which are so well-known that most anthologies include them.

### A CAST-OFF FAVORITE

*The dewdrops gleam on bright spring flowers whose scent is borne*
  *along;*
*Beneath the moon the palace rings with sounds of lute and song.*
*It seems that the clepsydra has been filled with the sea,*
*To make the long long night appear an endless night to me!*
                                    LI YI in Giles' version

## DESERTED

*Soaked in her kerchief with tears, yet slumber will not come;*
*In the deep dead of night she hears the song and beat of drum.*
*Alas, although his love has gone, her beauty lingers yet;*
*Sadly she sits till early dawn, but never can forget.*

Po Chü-i in Giles' version

It is noteworthy that longing here has not the impetuosity of Spring nor the density of Summer. It is thinning and toning down; but at the same time it has acquired a tenacity and an elasticity peculiar to Autumn. The longing seems to become longer and longer until it appears endless. In fact, I find in all the autumnal poets a tendency, more or less marked, to brood over their sorrows world without end. As Po Chü-i would say:

*Heaven and earth will pass away someday,*
*But this sorrow will linger on through all eternity!*

I am glad that I am not the only one to find in Autumn "a cadence, lingeringly long."

When we come to the last Season, we are confronted again with a different sentiment altogether:

*The willows grow in profuse confusion,*
*Screening off a secluded mansion.*
*The wails of the mango-bird in the morning*
*Fill the whole seraglio with sorrows.*
*From year to year, the flowers fall unseen,*
*And silently follow the Spring stream out of the moat.*

Sze-ma Tse

Not a trace of hope is to be found here. The heart is too faint even to yearn. What is the use of struggling when you are in the grip of ruthless fate? All the winter poets seem to wear taciturnity like an armor. Each seems to have made for himself a shelter to creep into, as a tortoise would withdraw into its impenetrable carapace in the face of a hostile world. Even when they were singing of the pleasures of life, as they occasionally did:

*Today we have wine, today let us drink!*
*Tomorrow will take care of its own sorrow!*

they remind me all too much of "the fowls of heaven," which, as
James Thomson says:

> *Tamed by the cruel season, crowd around*
> *The winnowing store, and claim the little boon*
> *Which providence assigns them.*

On the whole, fatalism is the common philosophy of the winter poets:

> *When time comes, all the forces of the universe are united to back you up.*
> *When luck is gone, even a hero cannot remain his own master.*

Another popular theme with the poets of T'ang is war. The following representative pieces, all of equal fame, will speak for themselves:

> *Sweet grape-wine filled in a cup of luminous jade!*
> *I want to drink on, but the cavalier's p'i-p'a is bidding me speed.*
> *Don't laugh, my friend, if I lie topsy-turvy on the sand!*
> *How many have ever returned from the battleground?*
>                                            WANG HAN

> *The commander-in-chief holds the banner in his hands,*
> *And starts out for the western front.*
> *The bugle blows at dawn,*
> *And a great army marches on!*
> *On all sides drums rumble like thunder,*
> *Arousing billows in the sea of snow;*
> *The troops howl in one voice,*
> *Causing the dark hills to tremble with fear.*
> *On the frontiers the martial spirit*
> *Rises to camp with the clouds,*
> *While on the battleground white bones*
> *Cling tenaciously to the roots of grass.*
> *Over the Sword River, blasts rage,*
> *And clouds roll in big masses.*
> *The stones on the desert are frozen;*
> *Even the horses sometimes slip to the ground.*
> *But the great general is dauntless in spirit,*
> *To him bitter hardships taste like sweetmeat.*
> *For he is sworn to requite the sovereign.*
> *By quelling the rebellious borders.*
> *Who doesn't see the glorious history of the past?*
> *But today we see a more glorious history in the making!*
>                                            TSEN TS'AN

*On horseback you will snatch fame and honor,—*
*A true Hero you, and worthy of your Manhood!*

TSEN TS'AN

*The old general of Kuan-hsi,*
*A good fighter he!*
*At seventy he is stout*
*As any youth could be!*

TSEN TS'AN

*Ten thousand drums sound like thunder,*
    *Making the earth rumble.*
*A myriad cavaliers hail forth like fire,*
    *Giving birth to a warm blast.*

KAO SHIH

*In front of the Peak of Happy Return*
*Lies a sandy desert, gleaming like snow.*
*Beneath the City of Victory*
*The moon spreads a frosty rug.*
*Hark! The notes of a reed-pipe!*
*Ah! Where comes the music?*
*In one night it fills a myriad hearts*
*With infinite yearnings for home!*

LI YI

*They swore to make a clean sweep of the Huns.*
*They started out with a will to die.*
*Five thousand men in furs and silk*
*Were all buried in a hostile desert land.*
*Ah, the pity of it! The skeletons*
*On the shores of the Inconstant River*
*Still live as darlings in the dreams*
*Of their brides in their nuptial beds!*

CHEN TAO

*Marshes, rivers and hills have all*
    *Become part of battleground.*
*How then are the people to live*
*By woodcutting and fishing?*

> *Tell me not, my friend, of winning*
> *Honors by the sword!*
> *The success of a single general is built*
> *Upon a myriad of skeletons!*
>                    TS'AO SUNG

Parting from our friends and dear ones is always a sad experience, especially in old China when the means of communication were very poor and the world seemed to be very wide indeed. Even Napoleon had said, "The moment which separates us from the object of our affections is terrible, it severs us from all the earth." And yet even this sadness has its seasonal modulations and nuances. In the first period, we find such sentiments as:

> *The existence of a single bosom friend on earth*
> *Turns the wide, wide world into a cordial neighborhood.*
>                    WANG PO

> *My friend took leave of me here at the Yellow Crane Tower,*
> *And went down eastward to Yangchow amidst the April vapors and*
>     *flowers.*
> *I strained my eyes and watched the shadow of the lonely sail vanish*
>     *into the blue hills.*
> *Now I see only the river flowing along the border of heaven.*
>                    LI PO, "On Seeing Off Meng Hao-zan"

In the second period, the sentiments are even more manly. Here some typical lines from Kao Shih:

> *Cleer up, dear friend!*
> *The present Emperor is full of "rain and dew."*
> *He will recall you soon from your temporary exile.*
> *Don't let our parting dishearten you too much!*
>                *   *   *   *   *
> *Don't feel sorry to be temporarily away from home.*
> *I know a man like you will find welcome wherever you go.*

In the third period, one feels a feminine touch and also a rather pale attempt to rationalize away the sorrows of parting. Here is what Yuan Chen said to his friend Po Chü-i:

*Last time we parted, it took us five years to meet again.*
*This time we part, who knows when we shall see my old pal?*
*Stay at peace, Lot'ien dear, don't miss me too much.*
*Just suppose I had not come to the capital at all.*

If Autumn is feminine, Winter is effeminate:

*True love looks like no love.*
*I only feel I cannot smile before the cup.*
*Even the wax-candle has a heart and pities our parting,—*
*It drops silent tears for us until the dawn.*
                                    Tu Mu

The third line needs some explanation. We call the wick "candle-heart." In this respect, our language is very much like Old English, which calls thought "breast-hoard," man "earth-dweller," jaundice "gall-disease," and the body "flesh-coat."

Even the dream-life of the poets seems to retain the qualities of the season to which they belong. What did Li Po dream? He tells us:

*One night I flew across the Mirror Lake in the bright moonlight!*

What did Tu Fu dream? He says:

*I dream of my native town, now overgrown with thistles and thorns;*
*I dream of His Majesty and his entourage, so near the beasts of prey.*

Another summer poet writes:

*On the pillow I had a wink and dreamed:*
*I walked all over the land south of the river.*

The dreams of the winter poets are apt to be nightmares. As Li Shang-yin has it:

*I dreamed I was setting out upon a long journey,*
*And was on the verge of being wrung from you,*
*I wept so hard that it was with difficulty*
*People succeeded to wake me up.*

As for the Autumnal period, I can find no better illustration than Yuan Chen's "Dreaming of a Well":

*In a dream I climbed to a high, high mound,*
*And on the mound I found a deep, deep well.*
*The climbing had made me tired and thirsty;*
*It was refreshing to look into the cool shaft.*
*Lingering around the well, I peeped into it*
*And saw my own face reflected in the spring.*
*I espied a pitcher in the well, now floating, now sinking:*
*But there was no rope to pull it to the well-head.*
*Apprehending that the pitcher would sink to the bottom,*
*I started wildly running to look for help.*
*I went into all the villages around the mound,*
*But found there were no men, but only fierce curs.*
*I returned and wept as I went around the well,*
*Crying aloud and then sobbing stifledly,*
*Till I was suddenly awakened from my dream,*
*Only to find a death-like silence around the house.*
*The candle flickered with a greenlight,*
*Which appeared liquefied through the prism of my tears.*
*A distant bell announced the midnight;*
*I could find no rest whether sitting up or lying down.*

*Suddenly I was reminded of the graveyard at Yen-yang,*
*With a vast expanse of wild fields around it.*
*The earth thick and the mounds heaped high,*
*And the dead buried in deep troughs.*
*Yet, although they are buried in deep troughs,*
*Their souls do sometimes communicate with the living.*
*Tonight my love who died so long ago*
*Transformed herself into a pitcher to make me alert.*
*Her thoughtfulness tapped the fountain of*
*My tears which have not ceased to flow.*
*My only grief is that there should be such a gap*
*Between the realms of dream and waking.*
*I know that someday I shall join her in the same grave;*
*But how long must I wait for this?*
*Besides I am afraid that disembodied souls*
*Might not recognize each other again.*
*With hopes and fears alternating endlessly in my mind,*
*I have sat listlessly till the dawn.*
*I have nothing to greet this beautiful spring morning*
*But these verses in memory of a dream!*

I can prolong this pageant of the seasons indefinitely. For on all conceivable subjects the poets seem to reflect the *Zeitgeist* of their particular period. It would, however, take a whole volume by itself to explain with some adequacy the causes of this phenomenon. One would have to look for them among the political, social, economic, literary-historical, biological, and psychological factors which all conspired together to make such a perfect year possible. But here I can only give some hints.

Ordinarily any movement in art and culture follows its own seasons. Some men of genius give the original impetus to it; then others come along and bring it to its fullest development; then a third group arrives upon the scene, curbing its exuberance and shaving off, with Occam's razor in their hands, all its superfluities, while preserving its beauties in neat form; and finally come the esthetes who, seized with the spirit of forms, give a finishing touch to the whole movement. But only on rare occasions do the internal seasons of such a movement run parallel with the seasons of life. And this is exactly what happened in the case of T'ang poetry. Its Spring coincided with the happiest days of the dynasty. Its Summer, while it did not see the fullest development of the dynasty, nevertheless saw its days of the most intensive and hectic activities. Rebellions had arisen and the centrifugal forces had been set loose, but then the centripedal forces were just as strong and great military geniuses like Kuo Tsu-i and Li Kwang-pi were leading the armies. It was an age in which Tsen Ts'an could exclaim:

*Today we see a more glorious history in the making!*

The poets were rather strengthened than disheartened by the great trials and hardships which they went through. But in the Autumn of T'ang poetry we feel an entirely different atmosphere. The troubled days had lasted too long for any candid optimism, and a sense of disintegration had entered the souls of the poets. As to its Winter, it happened to coincide with the fall of the great dynasty. So for once life and art seem to walk hand in hand, so much so that it almost looks like a lone instance of poor Leibnitz's "pre-established harmony."

Let us now proceed to Autumn.

# AUTUMN: PO CHÜ-I

The weather is cooling down, but not yet cold.
HAN WU

Where are the songs of Spring? Ay, where are they?
KEATS

New Philosophy calls all in doubt;
The element of fire is quite put out.
JOHN DONNE

But now the mystic tale that pleased of yore
Can charm an understanding age no more.
ADDISON

Outwardly conforming to the ways of the world,
Inwardly emancipated from all the ties of life.
PO CHÜ-I.

WRITING ABOUT the pine-trees, Po Chü-i (772–846) says:

In Autumn they whisper a soothing tune;
In Summer they yield a cooling shade;
In the depth of Spring the fine evening rain
Fills their leaves with little sparkling pearls;
At the close of the year heavy snowfalls

*Adorn their branches with unsullied jade.*
*From each season they derive a peculiar charm,*
*And this the reason why they are peerless among trees.*

I venture to think that the same is in some senses true also of the four seasons of T'ang poetry, and no one represents Autumn better than Po Chü-i himself. Like the pine-trees in Autumn, his poems, at least a great number of them, do whisper a soothing tune. But at this point, I must emphasize that the original word which I have rendered as "soothing" is *su*, which is very rich in meanings. In the first place, it means "sparse," as in Lao Tse's well-known sentence:

*All-embracing is heaven's net;*
*Sparse-meshed it is, and yet*
*Nothing can slip through it.*

Secondly, it also conveys the idea of being "detached" and "remote." When for example the relations between two persons are not very close we say that they are rather *su* to each other. Thirdly, as Dr. Lin Yutang has pointed out, it is connected with an idea which he translates as "mildness," but which I would translate as "flavorlessness." Fourthly, it has the meaning of "getting rid of impediments." When a tube is stopped up, we say we must *su* it. Lastly, it means "relieving the tension of your nerves," as when an old-fashioned Chinese doctor says to a patient, "Your case requires more *su* than *pu* (nourishment)." We Chinese use words more intuitively than logically. When we use the word *su*, all these meanings are more or less present in our minds. Some of them may float in the upper parts of our psyche while others may lurk just below the threshold of consciousness, but the point is that they are all stubbornly there. My English vocabulary is so limited that I cannot find any equivalent of this word. To put it clearly, a "*su* tune" is one that is sparse and thin of texture, mild or flavorless in its tones, detached and remote in its motif, fluent and unimpeded in its flow, and, finally, soothing in its effects. I am rather surprised to find that Arthur Waley, whom I regard as the best translator of Chinese poems, and who is especially happy in his translations of Po Chü-i, should have rendered the phrase as "a vague tune." Its meanings are indeed rather vague, but it does not mean "vague." I thought of the word "airy," which comes near to it, but it may also mean "sprightly" and "superficial," and you can say nothing of that sort about Autumn. I must confess that this word *su* has been haunting me for years, because it seems to me to furnish one of the keys to the understanding not merely of the poetry of Po Chü-i, but of the spirit of Autumn.

I feel that Po Chü-i would have agreed with me that he belongs to Autumn. For the qualities he ascribed to his own poetry all fall under the definition of *su* as I have given above, and therefore may by his own consent be called autumnal. Here is what he says about his poetry:

> *Laziness reinforced by illness gives me much leisure.*
> *What do I do with these idle days?*
> *Unable to discard the inkstone and brush,*
> *I still compose a poem now and then.*
> *But my poems are without color or flavor,*
> *A thing of derison to many.*
> *Superior people are put off by the flat meter;*
> *Common people mock at the plainness of word.*

In other words, his poetry is anything but thick and dense, anything but gorgeous and loud, anything but flowery and highfalutin, anything but enthusiastic and keen. It is akin to the old harp, which he says:

> *My lute is of cassia-wood with silken strings.*
> *Within it lie ancient melodies.*
> *The ancient tune is simple and quiet,*
> *It does not suit the modern man's taste.*
> *Fresh color is faded from the jade stops;*
> *Old dust has settled on the rose-red strings.*
> *It has long since it fallen into desuetude:*
> *But its sound is still refreshingly cold and clear.*
> *I do not refuse to play it for you,—*
> *But would people be willing to listen?*

He has not the rapturousness of Li Po nor the breathless intensity of Tu Fu; but he is full of subdued charm and mellow wisdom. On the whole, no poet seems to embody more perfectly than Po the spirit of Autumn, at least Autumn as Keats describes it so *su*-ishly in his "The Human Seasons." The sonnet is so appropriate to my present theme that it is worth quoting in its entirety:

> *Four seasons fill the measure of the year;*
> *There are four seasons in the mind of man;*
> *He has his lusty Spring, when fancy clear*
> *Takes in all beauty with an easy span:*
> *He has his Summer, when luxuriously*
> *Spring's honied cud of youthful thought he loves*
> *To ruminate, and by such dreaming nigh*
> *His nearest unto heaven: quiet coves*
> *His soul has in its Autumn, when his wings*
> *He furleth close; contented so to look*
> *On mists in idleness—to let fair things*
> *Pass by unheeded as a threshold brook.*
> *He has his Winter too of pale misfeature,*
> *Or else he would forego his mortal nature.*

What quiet coves Po Chü-i has in his soul can be gathered from these lines:

> *The peace of mind depends not on space;*
> *My room is no more than ten foot square.*
>              \* \* \* \* \*

> *Do you think that the cup of wine*
> *We drank this morning has instilled joy into my heart?*
> *This is a joy that springs from an inner fountain,*
> *Which the world will never understand.*

As to furling his wings, why, he even thinks his feet unnecessary:

> *So long as the mind is active,*
> *There is little use for the feet.*

Addressing himself to a crane, he says:

> *People love to see you dance,*
> *But I like you better standing still.*

His philosophy of contentment and his love of idleness are well known. Out of over three thousand six hundred poems he has left behind him, two-thirds of them seem to harp upon the same string. But here we must content ourselves with a few typical specimens:

# PLAIN TALKS TO MY NEPHEWS AND NIECES

*The world slights the unlettered:*
*I, happily, am no stranger to the letters.*
*The world slights those who hold no office:*
*I, happily, hold a high rank.*
*The old are often ill and miserable:*
*I, happily, have not an ache or pain.*
*Age is often burdened with worries:*
*I, happily, have no more dependents still unmarried.*
*My mind is at peace, not likely to be perturbed.*
*My body enjoys calm vigor, not sapped by external entanglements.*
*Hence it is that now for ten years*
*Body and soul have enjoyed leisurely peace and freedom,*
*Besides, in the declining years,*
*My desires and needs are reduced to a modicum.*
*A single fur robe to warm me through the winter;*
*One meal to keep me from hunger for the whole day.*
*Don't say that my house is small;*
*After all, one cannot sleep in more than one room.*
*What is the use of having many horses?*
*Can anybody ride on two backs?*
*Among the people of the world, perhaps seven out of ten*
*Are as fortunately situated as I am.*
*But not one out of a hundred*
*Is as contented as I am at heart.*
*In judging others, even a fool can see very clearly.*
*But in appraising their own situation, even sages can err.*
*Here I am not presuming to criticize others:*
*I am only speaking candidly to my next of kin.*

# THE LAZY MAN'S SONG

*Having an office, I am too lazy to fill it.*
*Having land, I am too lazy to farm it.*
*My house leaking, I am too lazy to repair it.*
*My clothes worn out, I am too lazy to darn it.*
*I am even too lazy to drink the wine in the cup;*
*It is the same as if it were empty.*
*I am too lazy to play the lute;*
*It is the same as if it had no strings.*

*When my folks tell me we have no more rice,*
*I am too lazy to grind the grains for cooking.*
*When letters from relatives and friends arrive,*
*I am too lazy to open them.*
*I have often heard it said that Hsi Shu-yeh*
*Passed his whole life in complete idleness.*
*Yet even he played his lute and worked at his forge.*
*He does not match me in supine laziness!*

## SELF-CONSOLATION

*Do not try to recall the past:*
*To recall it will only breed sorrows.*
*Do not try to anticipate the future:*
*To anticipate it will give rise to yearnings.*
*Better by day to sit like a doll in your chair;*
*Better by night to lie supinely in your bed.*
*When food comes, open your mouth!*
*When sleep comes, close your eyes!*
*These two things are, indeed,*
*The most pressing needs of your body.*
*As for the ups and downs, short life and long life,*
*Dismiss them from your mind and leave then to Providence.*
*One luxury I still enjoy: whenever the spirit moves,*
*I sing a mad song over a cup of wine.*

## A MIDDLE-CLASS RECLUSE

*High-class recluses stay in the government and market-place.*
*Low-class recluses enter into hills and woods.*
*Hills and woods are too lonely and isolated.*
*The court and the market are too much of a hustle and bustle.*
*I prefer to be a middle-class recluse,*
*Hiding myself in a sinecure!*
*Somewhere between society and solitude.*
*Neither busy nor idle.*
*No onerous work, mental or physical;*
*And yet no danger of hunger or of cold.*
*Throughout the year, no duties arise;*
*From month to month, salaries come.*
*If you want to roam and climb,*
*There are the Autumn hills on the southern suburb.*

*If you want to promenade and picnic,*
*There is the Spring garden east of the city.*
*If you are inclined to drinking,*
*You can go to the parties from time to time.*
*There are many scholars in Loyang,*
*With whom you can pass your time in pleasant chats.*
*If you are inclined to enjoy solitude and sleep,*
*You can shut yourself in as long as you want.*
*I can assure you no office-seekers or job-hunters*
*Will ever come to disturb your peace.*
*During our brief sojourn in this world,*
*It's hard to have everything to our heart's satisfaction.*
*If you are humble and poor,*
*You suffer hunger and cold.*
*If you are too high up and well off,*
*You will be eaten up by worries and cares.*
*Between adversity and prosperity,*
*Between opulence and penury,*
*A middle-class recluse*
*Steers safely through the channel of life.*

Of his willingness to let the fair things of life pass by unheeded, the
evidence is just as overwhelming:

*The willows are aging.*
*Spring is past its prime.*
*The sun is slanting.*
*What if the catkins are flying over the walls*
*To our neighbours' homes?*
*Who can always play the children's game*
*Of pursuing the catkins wafted in the Spring wind?*

### ON LOSING A SLAVE-GIRL

*My garden is only enclosed by a low wall,*
*With no census pasted on the gate.*
*Your escape makes me ashamed of my lack of kindness.*
*But what is past is beyond recalling.*
*A caged bird owes no allegiance to its owner.*
*A wind-tossed flower can cling to no twig.*
*Where is she staying tonight?*
*No one knows except the moonlight!*

## THE SPRING RIVER

*Heat and cold, dusk and dawn, wheel round without cease.*
*Before I am aware of it, two years have passed since I came to Chungchow.*
*In my secluded house, I hear only the morning and evening drum.*
*On the belvedere I gaze at the ships that come and go.*
*The song of the oriole lures me to promenade under the flowers.*
*The color of the grass invites me to sit beside the pond.*
*The only thing that gives me a perennial delight to contemplate is*
*The spring river eddying around endless pebbles and rocks.*

All this may lead us into thinking that Po is a real optimist. Here, you will say, is a man who has set himself completely in tune with life. Here we have at last found a philosopher who "could endure the toothache patiently." Doesn't he style himself as "Lot'ien" or The Optimist? But wait! The matter is not half so simple as this. The fact that the moon always shows its bright side does not mean that it has not also got a dark side. In the case of Po, moreover, he has not succeeded so well as the moon in hiding the less pleasant aspects. The very fact that he calls himself an optimist shows how pessimistic he really is. The long and short of it is that neither the word *su* nor Keats' lines constitutes a complete picture of Autumn. I would go so far as to say that they have only given us the more superficial aspects of Autumn, but have not touched its heart-strings. For Autumn is the saddest of the seasons. As Ou-yang Hsiu puts it so well: "Her breath is shivering and raw, pricking men's skin and bones; her thoughts are desolate, bringing emptiness and silence to the rivers and hills." It is rightly called "the doom-spirit of heaven and earth," or, as Horace would have it, "the harvest-season of the Goddess of Death." Never do life and death come so near as in Autumn. Its very fruitfulness hastens death. Its very fairness breeds sadness. One feels with William Watson:

*O be less beautiful, or be less brief!*

In one word, it is the season in which the dialectical process of Nature comes to a head. It is the clearing-house of the year, in which balances must be made up in cash, for the debt has ripened beyond cavil and its payment can no longer be deferred.

Yes, desolation is the soul of Autumn, and the door through which Po Chü-i enters into it is high awareness of the dialectical process of

Nature. The very first poem preserved in his complete works, which was written when he was fifteen, marks him down as an autumnal poet:

> Thick, thick, the grass on the plain!
> Each year, it has its season of growth and season of decay.
> No prairie fire can destroy it root and all;
> For when the Spring wind blows, it grows again.
> Its fresh smell, wafted from afar, invades an old road.
> Its bright emerald borders upon a desolate city.
> Once again it has come to see the genie of Spring off,
> With its heart seething with parting sorrows.

The second line reminds me of that wonderful passage of Ecclesiastes which begins with "To everything there is a season, and a time for every purpose under heaven." And the tone of the whole poem makes me think of Wordsworth's:

> Clouds that gather round the setting sun
> Do take a sober colouring from the eye
> That hath kept watch o'er man's mortality;
> Another race hath been, other palms are won.

The more I follow the seasons in T'ang poetry, the more I am convinced that, while the ages of life do influence an individual to some extent, yet the individual as a whole is destined to belong to a particular season. A springlike spirit will remain springlike even on his deathbed, and likewise an autumnal spirit begins to see and feel Autumn pretty early, if he is really not born autumnal. The child, as people say, is father to the man. In this connection, Alfred de Vigny has thrown out one of the keenest insights into human nature: "I have observed that everyone has naturally the character of one of the ages of life, and retains it always."

It seems to me that the vision of the interpenetration of opposites permeates the poetry of Po. He is by nature a Taoist. It's all very true that he "utilized Confucianism to order his conduct, utilized Buddhism to cleanse his mind, and then utilized history, paintings, mountains, rivers, wine, music and song to soothe his spirit." But this is exactly what only a thorough-going Taoist could have done. At any rate, the Tao Teh Ching and The Book of Changes seem to furnish the very sinews for the philosophy of Po. He expresses it very clearly:

*As the ancient sages have said,*
*Loss and gain follow in endless chain.*

And here is a song of opposites:

### GOOD AND EVIL

*We plant the orchids, but not the weeds;*
*And yet where the orchids grow, there grow the weeds.*
*Their roots and seeds are inseparably mingled;*
*Their stalks and leaves are inextricably entangled.*
*The sweet scent of the one and the bad smell of the other*
*Are indistinguishably mixed together.*
*To cut off the weeds would cause the orchids to perish:*
*To water the orchids is the weeds to nourish.*
*My mind is held in suspense between the two possibilities,*
*For both of them are attended with undesirabilities.*
*You are a wise man, my dear friend,*
*You may be able to solve this puzzle of my mind.*

This vision of the permeation of good and ill in life haunts him so persistently that it would crop up even in the most unexpected places:

### PLAYING WITH CHILDREN

*My niece is six years old;*
*I call her "A-Kuei."*
*My daughter is three;*
*I call her "A-Lo."*
*One is just beginning to talk and laugh;*
*The other can already recite poems and songs.*
*In the morning they play clinging to my feet;*
*In the night they sleep pillowed on my clothes.*
*Why, children, did you come so late,*
*When I am in my declining years?*
*By nature the young crave for affection;*
*And an old man's heart brims with paternal tenderness.*
*When the wine is at its sweetest, it turns sour.*
*When the moon is full, it begins to wane.*
*So with men the bonds of love and affection*
*Are the seeds of sorrow and care.*
*But all the world shares the same law.*
*How could I alone expect to be free from it.*

This calls to mind a stanza in Shakespeare's *The Rape of Lucrece*:

> *Unruly blasts wait on the tender spring;*
> *Unwholesome weeds take root with precious flowers;*
> *The adder hisses where the sweet birds sing;*
> *What virtue breeds iniquity devours:*
> *We have no good that we can say is ours,*
>    *But ill-annexed Opportunity*
>    *Or kills his life or else his quality.*

At this point I must make an explanation. I had said that Shakespeare was springlike, and then dealing with Tu Fu I said that Shakespeare was summery. Now I find myself comparing him with an autumnal poet! Furthermore, did I not write the essay on "Shakespeare as a Taoist"? The conclusion seems to be unescapable that Shakespeare belongs to Autumn! *Mais non!* My present view is that he is springlike in his heart, but autumnal in his head, and that's why he is so perfectly summery. As to Po Chü-i, it's an entirely different story. He is autumnal through and through, in his heart as well as in his head. For the dialectical process has two ends to it. One end leads to Heaven, the other to Hell. Shakespeare sees more of the bright side, and Po Chü-i more of the dark. The dark moments of Shakespeare are like the eclipses of the sun, which will finally shine forth again in all its effulgence. His best sonnets all testify to this eloquently. I wish especially to refer the reader to Sonnets **XXX** and **XXXIII**; and I cannot refrain from quoting this one in full:

> *When, in disgrace with fortune and men's eyes,*
> *I all alone beweep my outcast state*
> *And trouble deaf heaven with my bootless cries*
> *And look upon myself and curse my fate,*
> *Wishing me like to one more rich in hope,*
> *Featured like him, like him with friends possess'd,*
> *Desiring this man's art and that man's scope,*
> *With what I most enjoy contented least;*
> *Yet in these thoughts myself almost despising,*
> *Haply I think on thee, and then my state,*
> *Like to the lark at break of day arising*
> *From sullen earth, sings hymns at heaven's gate;*
> *For thy sweet love remember'd such wealth brings*
> *That I then scorn to change my state with kings.*

Love is his idol and prop. It is very significant that while he despises himself for his low spirits, Po is ashamed of his emotions! Here is a typical poem:

### AWAKENED FROM THE DREAM OF LIFE

*In the morning I weep over the death of a friend,*
*In the evening I weep over the death of a relative,*
*Friends and dear ones having passed away,*
*What is the use of my surviving alone?*
*The infinite ties of flesh and bone*
*Have raveled up my bowels into a knot of pain.*
*The accumulated affections of a life-time*
*Are turned into sour snuffles at the tip of my nose.*
*Griefs have enervated my limbs,*
*Weeping has dizzied my eyes.*
*In age I am only forty,*
*But at heart I am like a man of seventy.*
*I hear that in Buddhism they have a doctrine*
*Called "the Door of Emancipation":*
*Turn your heart into a still water,*
*Regard your body as a floating cloud;*
*Strip off your dust-stained clothes,*
*And tear yourself from the whirl of life and death.*
*Ah, why should one cling to the love of bitterness?*
*Why linger and loiter in the labyrinths of the world?*
*Upon deliberation, I make a solemn vow:*
*I vow that this temporary body of mine*
*Shall only receive the consequences of my past karma,*
*But I shall never sow any seeds for future crops of woe!*
*I swear I shall wash away the annoying dust*
*With the waters of wisdom and grace,*
*So that I may be spared from reaping sorrows and griefs*
*From the seeds of affection and love!*

Herein lies the difference between Christianity and Buddhism; Christ suffered in order to reap a crop of love, whereas the Buddhists, at least those of the type of Po Chü-i, dare not even love for fear of reaping a crop of sorrow. This also constitutes the difference between the West and the East. They espouse life whole-heartedly, but we try to play truant to it. Where Keats would say:

> *Welcome joy, and welcome sorrow,*
> > *Lethe's weed and Hermes' feather;*
> *Come today, and come tomorrow,*
> > *I love you both together!*

Po Chü-i would say:

> *To the happy ones the days seem to fly:*
> *For the sorrow-ridden the year crawls like a snail.*
> *Only he who is devoid of joy and sorrow*
> *Can take the long and short equally well.*

Where Keats says:

> *Fair and foul I love together,*

Po Chü-i answers:

> *Black and white I have ignored together.*

Where Keats asserts:

> > *. . . let me slake*
> *All my thirst for sweet heart-ache!*

Po would pour his cold waters upon this enthusiasm:

> *The Unicorn will be made into hash,*
> *And the Dragon into dried flesh.*
> *After all, the tortoise is not a fool:*
> *See how comfortably he trails his tail in the muddy pool!*

## THE ILLUSION OF LIFE

*Ever since my childhood days*
*Down till now when I am old,*
*My interests have varied with the years,*
*But the engrossment is ever the same.*
*Then, playing with sand, I built pagodas for the Buddha:*
*Now, tinkling with jade, I pay my homage to the Sovereign.*
*This and that are equally children's plays,*
*Unsubstantial shadows that pass in a moment of time.*
*Worldly ambitious do not lead to self-realization:*
*Non-attachment alone is the door to Truth.*
*I only fear that an over-eagerness in the pursuit of Truth*
*May indicate that one is still in the realm of illusion.*

A passionate nature preyed upon by the sense of desolation—that is Po Chü-i. He is most akin to Matthew Arnold, who, with all his smokescreen of "sweetness and light," is capable of sincerity in thought and expression, as in this:

> Ah, love, let us be true
> To one another! for the world, which seems
> To lie before us like a land of dreams,
> So various, so beautiful, so new,
> Hath really neither joy, nor love, nor light,
> Nor certitude, nor peace, nor help for pain;
> And we are here as on a darkling plain
> Swept with confused alarms of struggle and flight,
> Where ignorant armies clash by night.

To both Arnold and Po Chü-i, poetry ought in theory to be a criticism of life, but the best of their poems betray their precious theory, for they tell us in effect that life is not even worth criticizing! They seem to ask, *A quoi bon?* It is no accident that the very poem which all the competent anthologists regard as the best of Po, "The Song of the Lute-Girl," should have been spurned by himself as merely an occasional piece. For there we hear a cry of the outcasts in the air. There he is saturated through and through with the spirit of Autumn, and thus he is completely denuded. The denudation hurts his sense of dignity and self-respect. A stoic is caught crying like a child for a little toothache! No, no, he would protest, this is not my real mood, I am beside myself! But posterity has judged differently. Let us listen to the voice of Autumn:

### THE SONG OF THE LUTE-GIRL

> The other night I went down to the riverside
> To bid my friends farewell.
> Maples and rushes all around,
> Enchanted by Autumn's deathly spell.
>
> Dismounting from my horse, I found
> My guests on the point of starting.
> We drank some cups of wine in a cheerless mood,
> For no music was there to soothe our parting.

*The more we drank, the deeper we sank in despair;*
*For every cup brought our parting nearer.*
*At last, as I rose to say goodbye,*
*I saw the moon's pale face reflected in the watery mirror.*

*Suddenly we heard the sound of a lute on the waters,*
*Which gave us such a thrill in the heart*
*That I forgot to return,*
*And my guests were loathe to part.*

*We traced the sound and called out aloud,*
*"Hey, who is playing the lute?"*
*The music stopped at once,*
*And the musician remained for a long time mute.*

*At last, the voice of a lady answered,*
*And we moved our boat nearer hers.*
*We invited her to come over to our boat*
*In the hope that she would play for us.*

*We relit the lamps,*
*We called for more wine,*
*We renewed our feast*
*In a more cheerful state of mind.*

*But she was so modest and shy*
*That we had a hard time getting her to play.*
*Even then she still held her lute like a screen,*
*Behind which her face was half hidden away.*

*Then tuning up, she deftly turned the nuts,*
*And gave the strings a flying touch here and there.*
*The few scattered notes already had atmosphere,*
*Though they had not formed into an air.*

*Every string was charged with subdued emotion,*
*And every sound pregnant with thought,*
*As if she had breathed her soul into the lute,*
*Till it echoed the pathos of her life's unhappy lot.*

*With bent head and nimble fingers,*
*She played on with such gusto and flair*
*That the infinite hoard of her breast*
*Seemed to be laid bare.*

*Now a light skirmish, now a long-drawn dash:*
*Now a flying skip, now a violent snatch.*
*After "Robes of Cloud" she played a popular tune:*
*In her hands, the old and new seemed well to match.*

*The base tones grumbled like a sudden storm.*
*The trebles murmured like the whisper of a lover.*
*Then hoarse and shrill at once,—Oh, what a shower*
*Of pearls, big and small, upon a jade laver!*

*Anon an oriole, intoxicated with the flowers,*
*Pouring out the melody of her carefree soul!*
*Anon a streamlet sobbing stifledly*
*As it trickled through the shoal!*

*Then the flow stopped as if it had crystallized into ice,*
*And there ensued a pause oozing with hidden sorrows,*
*Sorrows that lie too deep for music to utter.*
*Oh, what Divine Silence, from which all music its meaning borrows!*

*With a plump we were roused from our trance, as though*
*A silver vase had burst abruptly into bits,*
*And the pent-up waters gushed out with all their force!*
*Or was it the mailed horsemen giving each other deadly hits?*

*A deadening peal of diapason ended all,*
*Like the ruthless ripping of silk out of boiling spite!*
*Silence on all sides: not a sound stirred the air.*
*We only saw on the river the moon shining white.*

*Then, with a sigh, she thrust her plectrum beneath the strings;*
*Smoothing out her robe, composing her mien, she rose from her seat.*
*"I was born and brought up," she said, "in the Capital,*
*Living in the southern part of the city, at the Musicians' Street.*

*"At thirteen, I had learned to play the lute:*
*My name was listed among the primas of the day.*
*My art won the applause of the maestros,*
*While my beauty was the envy of many a flower of yesterday.*

*"Young gallants vied with each other to win my favor:*
*A single song brought countless bales of red gauze.*
*Gold bodkins and silver pins were used to beat time and smashed;*
*Often the wine was spilt, staining my crimson new blouse.*

*"From year to year, life was one continuous smile for me.*
*Spring breeze and Autumn moon swept over my carefree head.*
*Then my brother went to the wars and my mother died:*
*With the passing of days my own beauty began to fade.*

*"My visitors diminished till carriages were rarely seen at my door.*
*I became a trader's wife when age had stolen upon me.*
*The trader thinks much of gains but little of partings:*
*Last month he went to Fu-liang to buy tea.*

*"I am left alone in an empty boat wafting on the river,*
*With nothing but the bright moonlight and cold waters around me.*
*In the depth of night I relive my youthful experiences in my dreams,*
*Waking to find my couch drenched with my tears of ennui."*

*"Already moved by the music of your lute," I responded,*
*"Your story has pierced my heart with a personal note:*
*For we are both castaways on the sea of life,*
*And a casual meeting has found us in the same boat!*

*"Since I left the Capital last year,*
*I have lived as an exile in Hsün-yang.*
*Illness and depression has taken hold of me.*
*And throughout the year I have not heard a song.*

*"I have made my home by the marshy river-bank*
*Surrounded by yellow reeds and stunted bamboos.*
*I have heard nothing but the gibbons' wailings,*
*And the heart-rending notes of the cuckoos.*

*"In the fine days of Spring and moonlit nights of Autumn,*
*I drank all alone without the slightest feeling of cheer.*
*And the hill songs and rural pipes*
*Conveyed no meaning to my ear.*

*"But tonight your heavenly music*
*Has regaled my spirit through and through.*
*Refuse not to play one more tune for me,*
*And I will write a song for you."*

*Touched by my words, she resumed her seat,*
*And hit upon a minor key so desolate and forlorn*
*That all the hearers wept, and I most bitterly of all,*
*Until there was not a dry stitch on my gown.*

# AUTUMN:
# MINOR POETS

*I wonder where on the desolate sea of life*
*The Muse is wailing the Autumn wind from year to year.*
                                        Li Ho

*I sing because my sorrows lie too deep for tears.*
                                    Liu Chung-yuan

*My drunken features are like the leaves of maples:*
*Though they are red, they are not Spring.*
                                        Po Chü-i

*Autumn wins you best by this, its mute*
*Appeal to sympathy for its decay.*
                                    Robert Browning

*Deep thoughts are decked by clearness.*
                                    Vauvenargues

It is significant that the music of the lute-girl should have ended in a minor key. If we compare Po Chü-i's song with Crashaw's version of "Musick's Duell," it would look very anemic indeed. But just here lies the secret charm of the autumnal poets, for they have a way of turning an anti-climax into a real climax! To them the sauce, not the fish, is the thing.

The truth is, poets are like sensitive barometers that reflect the slightest changes of the weather. The poets of this season were living in an age of decline, and it would not be sincere for them to sing in a major key. The age was rotten to the core. Po Chü-i saw no less than eight emperors on the throne; two of them were murdered by their trusted eunuchs; one died in consequence of taking the Elixir of Life; another was a usurper who had killed his brother, the rightful heir apparent; and the rest were all wretched middlings. Political intrigues were rife, and border troubles and internal disorders became the order of the day.

In his "Song of the Bitter Cold," Han Yu (768–824), consciously or unconsciously, seems to have reflected pretty faithfully the atmosphere of his age:

> Sinister blasts are disturbing the Universe,
> They are as sharp as a knife.
> The sun and the moon, powerful as they are,
> Are unable to breathe life into a dead toad.
> Ch'iu, Ch'iu, chirp the sparrows around the windows.
> They don't know their own smallness and insignificance.
> They lift up their heads to heaven and sing pleadingly.
> They want to live for a few more moments.
> It would be far better for you to be shot to death,
> Then at least you will have a taste of fire when you are roasted!

I cannot imagine either Li Po or Tu Fu writing in this vein. Nor would they have produced the following lines:

> The sky is jumping,
> The earth is stumbling.
> The cosmos has returned to Chaos.
> * * * * *
> The thunder-god chops
> The mountains into chips.
> The oceans are turned upside down.
> * * * * *
> With my face smeared with blood,
> I went to God in the dreamland.
> But at the gate of Heaven,
> I was scolded by the gate-keeper.

* * * * *

> *My heart is cold like ice,*
> *My sword white as snow.*
> *But unable to run my sword*
> *Through my slanderers,*
> *My heart has rotted,*
> *And my sword has snapped.*

I do not regard Han Yu as a good poet. I agree entirely with an old Chinese critic, Shen Kua that "Han Yu's poetry is prose in rhymes," although I must add that some of his prose writings, for example, that famous elegy on his nephew, may be called poetry without rhymes. This curious phenomenon arises because he does not seem to have taken poetry so seriously as he did prose. It appears to me that whenever he took to versification, he was in a frivolous mood, and regarded it only as a kind of literary acrobatics. He would sometimes, as in the "Song of the Stone-Drum," take in hand a dictionary of rhymes and try to show his resourcefulness by using almost all the words, however recondite and out of the way, under the same rhyme. He aims at "steepness" in language. To read his poetry is like watching a tight-rope dancer doing perilous feats over a yawning abyss. But poetry is no circus. Was he thinking of his art of poesy when he said:

> *I draw a snake and give it legs, to find I've wasted skill.*

But one thing is significant. As some keen critic has pointed out, Han Yu fed himself upon "the beauty of ugliness." It seems that he deliberately and with malice aforethought, as the lawyers would say, used words which are almost disgusting, such as "vomiting," "purging," "lice," "ulcer," "a rotten frog," and even "ordure." All this reflects the dirty age. "Where all is rotten," says the English philosopher F. H. Bradley, "it is a man's work to cry stinking fish."

But this is a man's work, not a woman's work; and Han Yu is the only masculine writer in this period of Autumn. All the other men respond to the environment in a more or less feminine way. They shied away from life, and found in art their only consolation and their only shield against the sordid perils of actual existence. Disgusted with life, they withdrew into themselves, and poetry became their dominant passion and remained their lifelong infatuation. Even as many-sided and moderate a man as Po Chü-i confesses to his weakness:

## SINGING MADLY IN THE MOUNTAIN

*Everybody has a special hobby:*
*Mine is in the composition of poetry.*
*Rid of all other ties of life,*
*This weakness still holds me in thrall.*
*Every time I come upon a beautiful landscape,*
*Every time I meet a dear old friend,*
*I would produce a poem and chant it rapturously*
*As though an angel had crossed my path.*
*Since my banishment to this marshy district,*
*I have lived half my time in the hills.*
*Whenever I have hit upon a new poem,*
*I would clamber all alone up the Eastern Slope,*
*Leaning my body on the banks of White Stone,*
*And keeping my hands to the branches of the green cassia.*
*When the hill and dale reverberate with my mad songs,*
*The apes and birds would peep wonderingly at me.*
*Fearing to become a laughing-stock to the world,*
*I resort to a place secluded from the sober crowd.*

He was madly in love with the muse, and he was afraid of becoming a laughingstock to the world. This is perhaps why he laid so much emphasis on the practical utility of poetry, just as a man who loves a girl for her sheer beauty would explain to his friends that she is a very able housekeeper as well. As a matter of fact, Po is a futilitarian masquerading as a utilitarian. But as we shall see, with most of the other poets in this period, their love for their mistress was much more open and unashamed. They would even kiss her in public! Let us see how they did it.

Chia Tao (788–843) brooded for three years over the wording of just these two lines:

*A lonely shadow walking at the bottom of the pond,*
*A body that hath often lodged amidst the woods.*

As a foot-note to these lines, he wrote a quatrain:

*Two lines of poetry in three years!*
*Each time I sing, two streams of tears!*
*If the understanding reader fails to smile and praise,*
*I'll to the hills and sleep away the rest of my days!*

Here is a man who ploughs his lonely furrow alone. But he was soon
to meet his friend Han Yu. Once he was riding on a donkey in the
streets of Ch'angan, and suddenly two lines flashed across his mind:

> *The birds nestle quietly in the trees by the side of a lake.*
> *A monk is knocking on a moon-lit door.*

Then he thought of changing "knocking" into "pushing," making unconscious gestures with his hands. He was so absorbed that he was not
aware that his donkey, apparently nonplussed by the unexpected
knocks, had stopped and was standing in the way of an officer's carriage.
He was arrested before the officer, who was none other than Han Yu.
Han asked him what he was doing with his funny gestures, and Chia
told him the whole story. Instead of punishing him, Han suggested
that the should retain the original word "knocking." That was the beginning of their friendship. More than a millenium has passed since
then, but even today I have just received a letter from a Chinese poet
of the old school, enclosing two poems and asking me politely to
"knock-push" them! Such is the continuity of the cultural life of China!
    Meng Chiao (751–814), another friend of Han Yu, whose position
among his friends, by the way, reminds me of that of Dr. Johnson,
wrote of himself:

> *I hum my poems all night long.*
> *Ghosts seem to be hovering around me and wailing with me.*
> *I wonder why I take poetry so seriously and will have*
>     *no rest.*
> *My soul seems to be bent upon wearing out my body like*
>     *a bitter enemy.*

Meng was not happy with the examiners, for he did not even suceed
in taking his first degree. A failure in life, he is, however, quite a success
in poetry. He sings of his poverty and adversity all the time. But what
else could he sing? Su Tung-po compares him to a hedge-cricket
shivering in the cold. But the Autumn of T'ang poetry would not be
complete without such mournful singers. The following are some of
his characteristic lines:

> *A man shivering in the cold*
> *Wishes to be turned into a moth;*

*For then he can fly to the luscious wax*
*To burn himself to death!*
     \*   \*   \*   \*   \*

*When the cold air enters the ulcers,*
*What a gnawing pain I feel in the night!*
     \*   \*   \*   \*   \*

*Too poor to get candles for the night.*
*I read my books in the bright moonlight.*
     \*   \*   \*   \*   \*

*When the rich take leave of each other,*
*There is sorrow in their faces.*
*But when poor people part,*
*Sorrows penetrate into their bones.*
     \*   \*   \*   \*   \*

*Always feeding on cheap vegetables,*
*My very viscera are bitter.*
*I force myself to sing,*
*But my song is without joy.*
*I meet obstacles wherever I go,*
*And yet people say that the Universe is wide!*

But it is on the strength of just one song that he has lived throughout all the generations and will continue to live in all the generations to come, "The Song of a Wandering Son":

*Thread in the hands of a doting mother:*
*Clothes on the body of a far-journeying son.*
*Upon his leaving, she adds one stitch after another,*
*Lest haply he may not return so soon.*
*Ah! How could the heart of an inch-long grass*
*Requite a whole Spring's infinite love and grace?*

I cannot imagine any anthology of Chinese poetry that does not include this simple hymn to motherly love. It introduces one to the Fifteen Mysteries of the Rosary:

*We are seeking for a mother*
*O'er the earth so waste and wide.*

It was not for nothing that William Cowper, another autumnal poet, who wrote "The Castaway," should also have written such tender lines about his mother. When the world is treating you like a step-mother, what is more natural for a child than to wish, with Alexander Pope (who is no less autumnal):

> To rock the cradle of declining age.

But how many persons possess such a privilege?

Another fanatical lover of the muse is Chang Chieh (circa 765–830), who is said to have burned a scroll of Tu Fu's poems, and, mixing the ashes with honey, taken a mouthful of it from time to time, saying, "This will change my viscera!" I don't know whether it had changed him, but it certainly had cleansed him in and out. It is always a delight to read his poems, or even to look at them. They are so very neat and pure. Every word is white jade. Of all colors he likes whiteness best, if we may judge by the frequency with which he uses the word "white." He never tires of speaking of the "white sun," "white silk," "white bones," "white hairs," "white atmosphere," "white China-grass," "white sand," "white waters," "white silver," "white water-lily," "white cloud," "white stork," "white stone," "white goblet," "white stamens," "white feathers," "white dew," "white ignana," "white dragon," and finally the "White Star." If he has not got the soul of Autumn, he has at least got its color. For according to a deep-rooted folk-lore of our country, Spring is green, Summer red, Winter black, and Autumn white. Autumn is like a middle-aged man who has seen so many colors in life that all of them begin to merge into white-ness, if not into colorlessness, as the colors of the rainbow vanish into nothing on "Newton's disc" when it is set a-rolling. And we must keep in mind that in Chang Chieh's time, the world was so muddy and bloody that one had only to look at it long enough to see a spontaneous vision of a quite different color arise before one's eyes, as in the case of crystal gazing. The same subtle reaction was at work when Tao Yuan-ming dreamed of the "Peach-blossom Fountain." He lived in a time when, as he testified:

> Darkening clouds hang over our heads;
> The showers of the season pour without cease.
> Not a streak of light in the skies above;
> Not a smooth road on the earth below!

But I wonder why George Meredith should have used "white" no less than thirteen times in his "Love in the Valley," which contains two hundred and eight lines in all. Was his time as dirty as the age of Chang Chieh? Or was it due to the queer *fin de siecle* feeling? I leave this little query to the students of English literature. In the meantime, here is a specimen from Chang Chieh.

### THE CHASTE WIFE'S REPLY

*Knowing well that I am a married woman,*
*You sent me for a gift a pair of bright pearls.*
*Moved by your tenacious love and devotion,*
*I fixed them on to my red silken vest.*

*But fair sir, I belong to a household of high honor,*
*My dear husband being a bulwark to the Royal Throne.*
*I know your love is as bright as the sun and the moon;*
*But I am sworn to serve my lord and my lord alone.*

*With tears flowing from my eyes, I return you the pearls.*
*Wish I had met you before the day of my wedding!*

Now what was the occasion of this poem? At that time, Chang Chieh was serving in the camp of a warlord, who was loyal to the emperor. Another warlord of doubtful fidelity sent him a letter and tried to entice him to his camp by a generous gift of money. He sent back the money and wrote him a letter enclosing this poem. A keen contemporary critic, commenting upon it, has observed that while this poem has two sides to it, the outer side and the inner, it can be enjoyed even without knowing the inner side. But what I want to point out here is that the desire to keep himself pure and chaste in the midst of a muddy world, so nicely expressed in this poem, seems to chime in perfectly with his preference for the white color.

Now we come to the greatest of the minor poets in the whole of T'ang, Li Ho, who was born in 790 and died in his twenty-sixth year in 816. It is said that he began to write poems as early as six years old, and very soon won the recognition of Han Yu. When still under twenty he went to the Capital to take the examination leading to the first degree of *chin-shih*. But those who were jealous of his talents objected to his being a candidate for *chin-shih* on the flimsy ground that his father's name was "Chin-su"! It's extremely absurd isn't it? How would you feel if people objected to your taking the Bachelor of Arts degree because your mother comes from a family of Batchelders? Han Yu took up his cudgels for his friend, and wrote a very eloqent defence. "If a son cannot be a *chih-shih* because his father is called 'Chih-su'," he argues, "then it would follow that a son cannot be a man if his father is called "'humanity'." Logically the argument is unanswerable, but it did not convince the examiners. It was an age of literary taboos, superstitions, inhibitions, and frustrations.

But Li Ho was a poetry-intoxicated boy. Every morning he went out on horseback, carrying his stationeries with him, and followed by a little slave with a silken bag on his back. Whenever the inspiration came, he would immediately jot down the lines on a slip of paper and throw it into the bag. In the evening, when he returned, he looked into the bag as a fisherman would look into his basket at eventide, and took out all the slips, arranging the isolated lines into stanzas and poems. It is said that he did this every day except when he was drunk or had to attend some funeral service in the neighborhood. Whenever his mother saw the bag full of slips, she would say tenderly but not without pain at heart, "This boy will not be satisfied until he has exhausted himself by pouring out his very heart into poetry!" Indeed, it is much easier to cut off the habit of opium-smoking than to tear oneself away from the grip of the muse. The muse is a jealous mistress, and no one can ever hope to win her heart, unless one pours out one's heart to her. In the case of Li Ho, the muse ate him up as the ferocious female mantis eats her mate! He died in his twenties, but he had completed the mission of his life. He had produced a type of poetry which has cut an indelible impression on the river of time. And our consolation is that he would have died more than two hundred years ago, even if he had lived as long as the fabulous Peng Chu. After all, we must remember that a poet is only a detour of nature to arrive at a few poems of lasting value.

Old critics of the highest standing have compared Li Ho with Li Po. Li Po, they say, is a fairy-like genius; while Li Ho is a ghostly genius. I endorse their judgment with all my heart, but nobody has ever pointed out that it is as impossible for Spring to produce a Li Ho as it is for Autumn to produce a Li Po. The truth is: another race has been, other palms are won. Let us see what kind of poems he writes:

*Glazed goblets*
*Of rich-colored ambers.*
*From the little plume*
*Wine flows in drops*
*Like dainty crimson pearls.*

*Dragons are cooked,*
*Phoenixes roasted.*
*Their grease and fat, jade-white,*
*Weep tears clean and bright.*

*Let's blow the dragon-flute!*
*Let's beat the iguana-drum!*
*Let the pearly teeth sing!*
*Let the slender waists dance!*

*Don't you see green Spring is near its sunset,*
*And peach-blossoms are falling like a shower of red rain?*
*Let's drink for a whole day!*
*Wine does not go down to the grave of Liu Ling.*

\*   \*   \*   \*   \*

*Autumn wold bright.*
*Autumn wind white.*
*The pool clear and deep.*
*Tse, tse, the insects chirp.*

*At the root of the clouds grows lichen,*
*Lending colors to the rocks on the hill.*
*The flowers are coldly red, weeping tears of dew,*
*Shedding around them an atmosphere of delicate sadness,*

*On the fields, wild and desolate,*
*Sprouts of rice are just shooting out like little forks.*
*Ah, it's Double Nine! Why have you come so late?*

*Somnolent glow-worms flit low*
*Across the dilapidated dikes.*

*Water flows in the veins of stone,*
*Washing out the sands one by one.*

Goethe has said that everything that is alive forms an atmosphere around itself. And what a ghostly atmosphere these poems shed! They send an eerie sensation down your spine.

*The corpse-candles look as if painted on the pine-trees,*
*Setting them afire with flowers!*

These flowers, blazing and gorgeous as they are, remind you of the
bright silver linings on a black coffin. A borrowed glory, yes; but the
very "borrowedness" is the property of Autumn. Sometime ago I had
a hunch which I have set down in verse:

*Spring challenges, Summer fights,*
*Autumn borrows, Winter steals.*

I have found that the works of Li Ho have confirmed my hunch so far
as Autumn is concerned. Here are some lines from Li Ho:

*Under the bright moonlight,*
*Autumn drops tears of white dew.*
\* \* \* \* \*

*Through the prism of tears, the lamp*
*Now brightens up, now flickers out.*
\* \* \* \* \*

*If heaven had the feelings of man,*
*Heaven itself would have grown old.*
\* \* \* \* \*

*The moon-lit dew drops crystal tears.*
\* \* \* \* \*

*My poetry envelops two strings of tears.*
\* \* \* \* \*

*The day is warm, but desolate is my heart.*
\* \* \* \* \*

*I am twenty but not happy,*
*My heart has decayed like a withered orchid.*
*Can youth be always young?*
*Even the sea may some day be turned into a mulberry field.*
\* \* \* \* \*

*All over the Autumn hillsides,*
*The mothers of the ghosts are wailing aloud.*
\* \* \* \* \*

*Ghostly rains are sprinkling an empty field.*
\* \* \* \* \*

*The ghosts are weeping, but a quoi bon?*
\* \* \* \* \*

*The marble stones on the hills*
*Are weeping transparent tears.*
* * * * *

*Let the peach-blossoms of Hsi Wang Mu*
*Bloom a thousand times,*
*And how many times Peng Chu and Wu Yen*
*Would have died?*
* * * * *

*Life is like a candlelight in a breeze.*
* * * * *

*Today the flag has burst into flowers:*
*Tomorrow will see the maple leaves wither.*

How all these lines remind me of Shelley's "Omens":

> *Hark! the owlet flaps his wings*
> *In the pathless dell beneath;*
> *Hark! 'tis the night-raven sings*
> *Tidings of approaching death.*

It may come as a surprise to readers, but I have found much affinity between Li Ho and Shelley. Chinese critics have pointed out that Li Ho is so fascinated by the pale ghost of death that he often writes his poems in the very rhyme of the word "death." I have found the same true of Shelley. But how is it that the total impressions of these two poets are so different from each other? My tentative answer is that Shelley is an autumnal spirit born in an age of Summer, an age in which he could absorb such hot stuff as the philosophy of Godwin; while Li Ho is autumnal in and out—both in his own heart and in his external environment, the future stretched out before him in desolate emptiness.

This period has so many poets—"teeming with rich increase," as Shakespeare would say—that I have to skip over many of them and give only a passing glance at a few others whom I cannot possibly omit. First there is Liu Chung-yuan (773–819), who, together with Han Yu, did for Chinese prose what men like Dryden, Swift, Addison and Goldsmith did for English prose, but who was also no mean poet. See how he wrote:

*Myriad mountains—not a bird flying.*
*Endless roads—not a trace of men.*

*Only an old fisherman in a lonely boat,*
*Angling silently in the river covered with snow.*

You cannot have a better picture of the soul of Autumn than this. And the language is an embodiment of steeliness. If Li Po wrote with a swan's feather, Tu Fu with a pen of gold, and Po Chü-i with a simple brush, Liu Chung-yuan, in prose as well as poetry, wrote with a bronzed stiletto.

Then we have Wei Yin-wu (circa 750–830), whom Chu Hsi has rated even above Wang Wei, being "more limpid, colorless, flavorless, and savorless" than the latter. Chu Hsi ought to have said that he is autumnal while Wang Wei is spring-like. Who but a child of Autumn could have written a political allegory like this:

*Alas for the lonely plant that grows beside the river bed,*
*While the mango-bird screams loud and long from the tall tree*
*   overhead!*
*Full with the freshets of the spring, the torrent rushes on;*
*The ferry-boat swings idly, for the ferryman is gone.*
                                                 GILES' version

A ferry-boat without a ferryman! That was the plight in which the ship of state found itself in his age. To a friend, he wrote:

*Last year when we parted the flowers were blooming.*
*Today I see the same flowers blooming again.*
*The events of the world are becoming more and more vague and*
*   unpredictable.*
*The sorrows of Spring have so darkened my spirit that I only want to*
*   sleep.*

Nor can we omit Liu Yu-hsi (772–842), who still lives by half a dozen of his poems. The best-known is also the most typically autumnal:

*By the side of the Red-Sparrow Bridge,*
*The wild grasses are bursting into flowers.*
*At the mouth of the Black-Clothes Lane*
*Are shining the slanting beams of the evening sun.*
*The swallows that used to frequent*
*The towering mansions of the erstwhile great men,*
*Now are flying into the humble homes*
*Of the ordinary people.*

Poetry is entering into a reminiscent mood, isn't it? But the most reminiscent of all is Yuan Chen (779–831), who has won immortality by
his elegies about his wife, which contain these unforgettable lines:

> I remember how you fumbled in the suitcases
> In order to find more clothes for me.
> I remember how I impelled you to pawn
> Your golden hairpin to change for more wine.
> * * * * *
> I have nothing but a winkless night
> Of memories and sighs to requite,
> A lifetime of hardships
> And ever-knit eyebrows.

Henry King in his "Exequy on His Wife" concluded with a hope:

> . . . I am content to live
> Divided, with but half a heart,
> Till we shall meet and never part.

But Yuan Chen was not so sanguine:

> To lie together in the cold grave,
> What does that amount to anyway?
> To meet you in our after life again
> Is a hope I dare not even entertain.

If Yuan Chen were living today, he would wonder why some men are
so anxious to divorce their wives when there is in store for them an
eternity of separation.

There are many poems on the tragedy of Ming Huang and Kuei-
fei. The longest is from the pen of Po Chü-i, the shortest is by Yuan
Chen. I like the latter even more than the former:

> A desolate old Traveling Palace.
> The flowers in utter loneliness blush.
> A white-headed maid-of-honor is there,
> Sitting idly and telling stories about Hsüan Tsung.

But I cannot bid goodbye to Autumn without mentioning an elder
contemporary of Po Chü-i, Chang Chi, who introduced Autumn and
set the tone to it by this remarkable poem which he wrote in a boat
temporarily moored in Soochow:

# WINTER:
# THE ANATOMY
# OF A MOOD

One must have passed through the tunnel to understand how black is its darkness.
SAINT THERESE OF LISIEUX.

> . . . Parting day
> Dies like the dolphin, whom each pang imbues
> With a new colour as it gasps away,
> The last still loveliest.
> BYRON

> Drag on, long night of winter, in whose heart,
> Nurse of regret, the dead spring yet has part.
> WILLIAM MORRIS

> How infinitely charming is the setting sun!
> Only it is so near the yellow dusk.
> LI SHANG-YIN

> The more I mumble my verses,
> The fainter grows my voice.
> CHANG CH'IAO

IN JAMES THOMSON'S "The City of Dreadful Night" I have run across two lines that are very much to my liking:

> O desolation moving with such grace!
> O anguish with such beauty in thy face!

The first line gives us a snapshot of the autumnal poetry we have just dealt with; the second forms a studied portrait of the soul of Winter. Autumn is desolate at heart but graceful in its motion: Winter is pent up with anguish within, but its external aspects are stunningly beautiful. Its blood is warm, but it assumes the appearance of a grandsire cut in alabaster. It is as angry as Summer, if not more so; but its anger is afraid to show itself,—"an impotent fury conscious of its impotence." It is like Vesuvius sweallowing its own lava. In a season like this, one no longer wishes to

> Rock the cradle of declining age.

On the contrary, one begins to lay blame at the door of one's parents:

> Ai, ai poor mother,
> Your birth-pangs were fruitless.

One is so disgusted with life that one could wish one's father had been a monk and one's mother a nun, or at least that they had been thoughtful enough to practice birth control:

> I wedded not in my life.
> Would my father had taken no wife.

One becomes a prey to suicidal thoughts:

> At the beginning of my life
> All was still quiet;
> In my latter days
> I have met these hundred woes.
> Would that I might sleep and never stir!

This was how a poet felt during the last days of the western Chou Dynasty, and this was how Sophocles must have felt when he indited these lines in his "Ajax":

> Oh! when the pride of Graecia's noblest race
> Wanders, as now, in darkness and disgrace,
>     when Reason's day
> Sets rayless—joyless—quenched in old decay,
>     Better to die, and sleep
> The never-waking sleep, than linger on,
> And dare to live, when the soul's life is gone.

To such a spirit, Spring, the life-giver, is the most unendurable season:

*April is the cruellest month, breeding*
*Lilacs out of the dead land, mixing*
*Memory and desire, stirring*
*Dull roots with spring rain.*

When one finds within oneself nothing but

*Blown buds of barren flowers,*

How the bright colors stab the heart!

*Oh, the flowers of the bignonia,*
*Gorgeous is their yellow!*
*The sorrows of my heart,*
*How they stab!*

The poets of different ages and different countries seem to feel the same way if they belong to the same season. Here is how Li Ch'ün-yu of the last period of T'ang describes Spring:

*Who can depict the soul of Spring?*
*Its brilliant colors breed vertigo in me.*
*The evening waters reflect the green sorrows of the poplars.*
*Behind a deep window one senses the sadness of the fallen flowers.*
*I think of the lonely harems, where the weather is warming up,*
*And the ocean swallows coming flying in pairs.*
*My autumnal thoughts bedim the radiant vapors;*
*A boundless fog fills the cup of the universe.*

When a gale is blowing, it brings profound trouble to the soul; and the greater the soul, the more intensely it suffers. As Pascal says, "Great men and insignificant men have like accidents, like vexations, and like passions; but the former are on the outside of the wheel, and the latter near the center, and are therefore less agitated by the same movements." And I should imagine that of all great men the poets are the most agitated, precisely because they live in a garret, if not in an ivory tower. Who has not occasionally felt as Goethe did, "What a time it is when we must envy the dead in their graves!" Or as Pushkin did:

*I've lived to bury my desires,*
*And see my dreams corrode with rust;*
*Now all that's left are fruitless fires*
*That burn my empty heart to dust.*

Fortunately, at such moments a poet would feel with a sense of relief that he has not long to wait

> *Till suddenly, Eternity*
> *Drowns all the houses like a sea.*

This thought alone saves him from committing suicide.

In Spring body and soul are undifferentiated; in Summer they are differentiated but live in perfect wedlock; in Autumn they begin to quarrel; and finally in Winter they are divorced, or one of them dies, leaving the other as its widow. If the body has died and the soul lives on, one achieves a real resignation of which the mellow wisdom of Autumn is but a pale shadow. The grapes are no longer sour, but the celestial fruits are infinitely sweeter. The soul has found its home, and all that it desires is to spend its heaven in doing good upon earth. Such a soul is a poem in itself and finds no particular urge to write verses. It becomes a note in the Grand Symphony of God. Its only wish is to see His Kingdom come, to see reality turned into poetry. It is so consumed by the flame of living love that it can at most utter an ecstatic cry as did Saint John of the Cross:

> *O burn that burns to heal!*
> *O more than pleasant wound!*
> *And O soft hand, O touch most delicate,*
> *That dost new life reveal,*
> *That dost in grace abound,*
> *And, slaying, dost from death to life translate!*

But such poets are rare and not necessarily of the highest order, for when one really feels ecstatic, when one's heart throbs in unison with the heart of the universe, silence becomes more musical than any song, and Shakespeare himself appears like a poor bird who sings in such profuse strains simply because he has not found his ideal mate.

In one sense, a poet like Saint John of the Cross belongs to no season; for, while he, too, has experienced Winter, the obscure night of the soul, as he calls it, he has passed through the dark tunnel and finds himself in a realm where the whirligig of time has stopped. Most poets of Winter remain in the cul-de-sac of the world. They feel as Li Shan-fu did:

*I faint from grief, but no tears come from my eyes;*
*Demented and maddened, I feel like one who has lost his soul.*

Their souls have died in agony or wandered away from them, but their
bodies still linger on like guests who have out-stayed their welcome.
Their problem is how to flirt with life and keep up their spirits during
the interval between their spiritual death and their physical death. The
problem belongs to the body exclusively, and body reasons—for it is a
great logician—in this way:

> *The wheel of life no less will stay*
> *In a smooth than rugged way:*
> *Since it equally doth flee,*
> *Let the motion pleasant be.*

The conclusion seems to be unescapable:

> *Crown me with roses whilst I live,—*
> *Now your wines and ointments give;*
> *After death I nothing crave;*
> *Let me alive my pleasures have!*
> *All are Stoics in the grave.*

Indeed, no one clings to life with such tenacity as an old man:

> *But this I know, without being told,*
> *'Tis time to live, if I grow old;*
> *'Tis time short pleasures now to take,*
> *Of little life the best to make,*
> *And manage wisely the last stake.*

The epicureans have a way of making all stoics look like fools:

> *There grows an elm-tree on the hill,*
> *And by the mere an alder-tree—*
> *You have a coat, but do not wear it,*
> *You have a robe, but do not don it,*
> *You have a horse, but do not ride it,*
> *And by-and-by you will die,*
> *And others will enjoy them!*
>
> *There grows a gum-tree on the hill,*
> *And by the mere a chestnut-tree.*
> *You have wine and food, why do you forget*

*Sometimes to play your lute,*
*Sometimes to laugh and sing,*
*To lengthen the day by feasting at night?*
*For by-and-by you will be dead,*
*And others will possess your house.*

Perhaps, if you have some conscience left, you will ask, "What heart have I to play the fiddle while Rome burns?" To which the devil will answer, "But what else can you do, my sophomoric friend?" And by and by you may find yourself singing:

*Hey nonny no!*
*Men are fools that wish to die!*
*Is't not fine to dance and sing*
*When the bells of death do ring?*
*Is't not fine to swim in wine,*
*And turn upon the toe,*
*And sing hey nonny no!*
*When the winds blow and the seas flow?*
*Hey nonny no!*

This is how a poet would feel in any decadent period, when the world is hopelessly at sixes and sevens. Tu Ch'iu-niang, whom we may regard as the mother of the Winter of T'ang Poetry, seems to have set the key to it in the following song:

*I would not have thee grudge those robes*
*    which gleam in rich array,*
*But I would have thee grudge the hours*
*    of youth which glide away.*
*Go pluck the blooming flower betimes,*
*    lest when thou com'st again*
*Alas, upon the withered stem no*
*    blooming flowers remain!*

It seems to me that Walter Pater sums up the wintry philosophy of life when he says, "Well! we are all *condamnés,* as Victor Hugo says: we are all under sentence of death but with a sort of indefinite reprieve —*les hommes sont tous condamnés a mort avec des sursis indefinis:* we have an interval, and then our place knows us no more. Some spend this interval in listlessness, some in high passions, the wisest, at least among 'the children of this world,' in art and song. For our one chance lies in expending that interval, in getting as many pulsations as possible into the given time."

It is very odd that the exponent of such a dead man's philosophy of life should also be so very wintry in point of style. As Samuel Butler puts it, "Mr. Walter Pater's style is, to me, like the face of some old woman who has been to Madame Rachel and had herself enamelled. The bloom is nothing but powder and paint and the odour is cherry-blossom." I feel the same about it, for it reminds me of a stanza in Lucianus' "Artificial Beauty":

> *You give your cheeks a rosy stain,*
> *With washes dye your hair,*
> *But paint and washes both are vain*
> *To give a youthful air.*

I have often thought that Spring is cosmically-minded, Summer historically-minded, Autumn philosophically-minded, and Winter cosmetically-minded. Lady Blessington has somewhere said that the best cosmetic for beauty is happiness. But the point is that happiness is not to be had for a song, and where it is entirely lacking, powder and paint are not altogether useless. To congratulate ourselves for not belonging to a decadent movement is one thing; but to declaim against it is quite another. There are times when artificiality is not only natural but inevitable, when Art, tongue-tied by authority, dares not deal with the grand issues of life, and decoration becomes its main activity and sole concern. Such periods deserve as much sympathy from us as the "posthumous coquetry" of a lady:

> *Let there be laid when I am dead,*
> *Ere 'neath the coffin-lid I lie,*
> *Upon my cheek a little red,*
> *A little black about the eye.*

Since to the wintry spirit everything is posthumous, a craftsman-like solicitude fares no worse than the noble negligences of a genius, and artificiality is no more a house of cards or a fabric of snow than nature itself. Even a brief recalescence of Spring is not out of place in this season of bitter cold. How nicely George Herbert, who belongs to the "Fantastic School of Piety" puts it:

*And now in age I bud again;*
*After so many deaths I live and write;*
*I once more smell the dew and rain,*
*And relish versing; O my only light,*
    *It cannot be*
    *That I am he*
*On whom thy tempests fell all night.*

If our life on earth is but a dream, as indeed it is, then the whiteness or colorlessness of Autumn is no less shadowy than the bright colors of Spring and Summer. Instead of annihilating all the colors, what about, as Andrew Marvell would have it,

*Annihilating all that's made*
*To a green thought in a green shade?*

These lines remind me of a beautiful stanza by a wintry poet of T'ang, Liu Teh-jen:

*A pair of white birds, oblivious of*
*The endless events of the dusty world,*
*Fly side by side and fade gradually*
*Into the faint emerald of the hills.*

Instead of the emerald dissolving into whiteness, we have here two specks of whiteness fading into the hill-formed emerald.

    It is very significant that the word "emerald," which we so often met in the poems of Tu Fu, but which all but disappeared in the poetry of Autumn, has come back again in this period of T'ang poetry. The variegated and full-blooded world which Autumn had annihilated seems to revive in Winter. And yet it is no longer the same world. The world that Winter has built upon the wrecks of Autumn belongs to an order of its own, it is bathed in the ether of imagination, it has a hieroglyphic veil of inscrutable mysteries drawn over it. Its symbol is not the sun or even the moon, but the candlelight. As Helen Waddell phrases it so beautifully, "One sees most by candlelight, because one sees little. There is a magic ring, and in it all things shine with a yellow shining, and round it wavers the eager dark. This is the magic of the lyrics of the 12th century in France, lit candles in 'a casement ope at night,' starring the dusk in Babylon; candles flare and gutter in the meaner streets, Villon's lyrics, these; candles flame in its cathedral

darkness, Latin hymns of the Middle Ages, of Thomas of Celano and
Bernard of Morlaix. For if Babylon has its Quartier Latin, it has also
its Notre Dame. The Middle Ages are the Babylon of the religious
heart." Miss Waddell might have added that the Winter of T'ang
Poetry is the Babylon of the heart of China. It, too, has its Quartier
Latin, in which many a "hermit of the green chamber" fritters away his
nights. It, too, has its Notre Dame: the lonely inn, in which a homeless
wayfarer confides his sorrows to an orphan-like candle that listens
sympathetically to him and weeps tears of blood over the sad story of
his life. A few specimens will suffice:

> *It has been so hard for us to meet,*
> *It will be harder for us to part.*
> *The East Wind is growing feeble;*
> *The flowers are beginning to fade.*
> *But the silkworm in the Spring goes on*
> *Spinning gossamer threads until its death;*
> *And the candle of wax ceases not to weep*
> *Its tears of blood until it burns itself to ashes.*
>                          LI SHANG-YIN

> *True love looks like no love.*
> *Only I cannot bring myself to smile before the cup.*
> *Even the wax-candle has a heart and pities our parting,—*
> *It drops tears for us until the dawn.*
>                          TU MU

> *The wax-candle weeps tears of blood,*
> *Lamenting the coming of the dawn.*
>                          LI SHANG-YIN

> *A lonely candlelight ushers in*
> *A Spring far away from home.*
>                          TS'UI TU

> *I sit and watch*
> *The flower-like moon*
> *And the sparkling stars*
> *Fade from the sky.*
> *The shadows of the mountains*
> *And the far echoes of the tides*

*Are weaving Sorrow in the gloom.*
*In the depth of night,*
*Before the candlelight,*
*The events of the past decade*
*Come flooding to my heart*
*Together with the rain.*

TU HSÜN-HE

*A flickering candlelight*
*Accompanies a dissolving dream.*
*The lands of Ch'u lie dimly*
*On the borders of heaven.*
*The moon has gone down,*
*And the nightingale has ceased its song.*
*All over the courtyard*
*Apricot flowers are flying.*

WEN T'ING-YÜN

*At midnight I wake from wine,*
*The red candle is burned almost to its socket.*
*Its cold tears have been congealed*
*Into a coral-reef.*

P'I JIH-HSIU

*I sit up and watch*
*The dim, dim flame*
*Of a lonely, lonely lamp*
*Flickering out noiselessly*
*Toward the dawn.*

CH'I CHI

We are no longer in the world of flesh and blood. We are in the dreamland in which the soul glimmers like the flame of a candle. The landscape has been transformed into an "inscape". The world is drowned in the immeasurable ocean of darkness, and there remains only "an odorous shade."

*An odorous shade lingers the fair day's ghost,*
*And the frail moon now by no wind is tost,*
*And shadow-laden scents of tree and grass*
*Build up again a world our eyes have lost.*

The most touching type of wintry poetry is where dead Spring comes back to life in a dream. Prince Li Yu, the last monarch of the Southern T'ang, who ended his days in captivity, is a consummate master of this genre of lyrics. I shall dedicate a whole section to the study of the life and works of this purest lyricist of China. Two samples will suffice here:

## A DREAM

*Ah, how sad!*
*Last night in my dream*
*I was again roaming in the Royal Park*
*Like in the old days—*
*Carriages were rolling like a stream*
*And horses prancing like dragons—*
*Moonlight flowers were quivering*
*In the warm caress of the Spring breeze!*

## UPON WAKING FROM A DREAM

*Outside the window-screen the rain drizzles and drips.*
*The Spring is gasping away.*
*Under thin silken quilts I shiver in the cold tide of the morning watch.*
*In a dream, forgetting my homeless plight,*
*I feasted myself like a glutton upon the past joys again!*
*Ah, lean not upon the balcony all alone,*
*Lest you should see the endless rivers and mountains,*
*That make separation so easy and meeting so hard!*
*The stream flows on, the flowers have fallen, and the Spring is gone,*
*Leaving no trace in Heaven or on earth.*

In his dreams he becomes a king again; upon waking, no such matter! He is like a widow dreaming of her hymeneal night. A volcanic cataclysm, a yawning hiatus, lies between the past and the present. Everything is gone, leaving no trace behind, like the ceasing of exquisite music. There seems to be an eternal gash on time, covered up only in dreams, but in effect cut deeper by them. How those lines remind me of Michael Field's "After Soufriere":

*It is not grief or pain;*
*But like the even dropping of the rain*

*That thou art gone.*
*It is not like a grave*
*To weep upon;*
*But like the rise and falling of a wave*
*When the vessel's gone.*
*It is like the sudden void*
*When the city is destroyed,*
*Where the sun shone:*
*There is neither grief nor pain,*
*But the wide waste come again.*

And yet something is haunting still, the fair day's ghost. A ghost! That's what Winter is. Autumn may be ghostly, but it is still a human being. Winter is a ghost, but what a lovely ghost! What a beautiful face and a kindly voice the ghost has! "Vainly you ask yourself:— 'Whose voice!—whose face?' It is neither young nor old, the face: it has a vapoury indefinableness that leaves it a riddle . . . yet you cannot ignore it, because of a certain queer power it possesses to make something stir and quiver in your heart,—like an old vague regret,—something buried alive which will not die." And the voice, though feeble as the hum of a bee, "exhales an exquisite perfume—strange, indistinct, and yet, after the manner of perfume, unforgettable." Spring is like the pink that buds and blooms so gayly in the arbor; Summer is like the rose with its damask dyes peering through a thick leafage; Autumn is like the lily unstained and chaste, or the violet wrapped in lonely communings; but Winter is like the forget-me-not, whose love alone can feed the lamp of pale existence. Spring is something to be seen; Summer can be tasted and touched; Autumn is to be heard; but Winter, like an odorous shade, can only be smelled. Spring liberates you; Summer inspires you; Autumn soothes you; but Winter captivates you. If the reader will excuse me for resorting to a homely analogy, I would say that T'ang poetry as a whole is like a good dinner, of which Spring is the soup and the fish, Summer the beefsteak or stuffed turkey, Autumn the ice-cream and the fruits, and Winter is the little cup of mocha that crowns all. Spring may be appetizing, Summer savory, and Autumn refreshing, but who can ever forget the fine flavors of the mocha?

Who but a winter poet like George Herbert would have thought of Spring as "A box where sweets compacted lie"? To the children of the other seasons this may look like a fantastic conceit; but Winter, as I have said, is cosmetically minded, and this kind of perfumed image arises spontaneously in its mental eye. In our father's year there are four seasons; and I have a suspicion that he is even more fond of Winter than the others:

> And so a flower bright
> Has bloomed in coldest winter
> E'en in the deepest night.

It may be that Winter is a peacock which, with its splendid plumage and tail, reminds you of a lady "in gloss of satin and glimmer of pearls." But only a shallow critic would say that a peacock is less natural than a skylark. There is a provision in the universe even for a pair of mandarin ducks in a golden cage. How touchingly Li Shang-yin has put it:

### ON THE MANDARIN DUCKS

> The hen has gone.
> The drake is flying
> All over the boundless sky
> In search of his love.
> He only sees
> The gauzy clouds,
> And his eyes
> Ooze with tears.
> Oh, have done with a life
> Amidst the winds and waves!
> Ah for a golden cage
> In which he and she
> Can live together
> In sweet thraldom!

To Li Po the universe is not big enough for his spirit to soar in: to Li Shang-yin a little corner is good enough for his body to live in, provided only that it is safe and secure from the cruel blasts of the north wind that are making a holocaust of the world. He feels somewhat, though not exactly, as Richard Lovelace does:

> Stone walls do not a prison make,
>   Nor iron bars a cage;
> Minds innocent and quiet take
>   That for an hermitage;

*If I have freedom in my love,*
*And in my soul am free,*
*Angels alone, that soar above,*
*Enjoy such liberty.*

Perhaps, Li Shang-yin feels more closely with Ovid, whom I regard as his contemporary and next of kin:

*I pray you, stay, Aurora; and to your Memnon's shade*
*A sacrifice—I vow it—shall every year be made.*
*'Tis now my love is by me, her lips are mine to kiss,*
*Her arms are twined about me—is any hour like this?*

Like Ovid, too, Li Shang-yin, fed up with the nature of things as they are, dives into the nature of things as they are fancied to be, and deals in occult metamorphoses:

## THE WEB OF LIFE

*The precious harp has fifty strings,*
*No more, no less.*
*How every string, every nut, evokes thoughts*
*Of my youthful days!*
*In his morning dreams, Master Chuang was metamorphosed*
*Into a butterfly!*
*The Spring heart of Prince Tu Yu of old still echoes*
*In the cuckoo's cry!*
*When the moon shines brightly on the murky sea,*
*Tears come from the pearls.*
*When the sun is warm, the jades of the Blue Fields*
*Send up smokes in curls.*
*A sudden glimpse into the mystery of mysteries flashed*
*Across my mind,*
*But its meaning escaped immediately, for like lightning*
*It struck me blind!*

How well William Blake seems to have sized them up, these winter poets:

*The Door of Death I open found,*
*And the Worm Weaving in the Ground;*
*Thou'rt my Mother, from the Womb;*
*Wife, Sister, Daughter, to the Tomb:*

*Weaving to Dreams the Sexual strife.*
*And weeping over the Web of Life.*

And yet many a dry-humored critic has said that Li Shang-yin is the most obscure poet of China and the above-quoted poem on The Web of Life is the most obscure of his poems. They have even given him a nickname: "an otter offering libations to the fish!" That is, they could not make head nor tail of his poems. But what do they know about poetry, especially when it has reached its stage of imago? They don't realize that the poems of this stage are like women in that they are made to be loved, not to be understood. I would even go as far as to say that the only way of understanding them is by not trying to understand them. Simply love them, and they will confide their secrets to you; and this usually happens when you are not particularly interested in knowing them, for you want to go to sleep. Oh the charm of the *ewige Weiblisch,* the eternal feminine, the living embodiment of the irony of life which is the very stuff of universe! How shallow the masculine looks beside it! A hairpin on the head of a woman shoots beyond the barriers of the unknown, while all the philosophies of men have only served to mystify existence. All roads lead in the end to the cosmos, but cosmetics may be a short-cut. Nature herself seems to me a great coquette.

Winter is woman. She lives and moves and has her being in the realm of essence. She is emancipated from the phenomenal world. She has her own system of causality, and she has a way of interfusing the senses with one another. At her magic touch even the barriers between matter and mind seem to have crumbled. What kind of a world she lives in can be gathered from the few glimpses the following specimens furnish us:

*A lamp glimmers amidst a choir of crickets.*
LI CH'ANG-FU

*My lingering thoughts have reddened the maple leaves.*
Prince LI YU

*The west wind is scattering sorrows among the green ripples.*
Prince LI CHIN

*All alone I have been blowing the pipe of jade*
*Until my little garret freezes with its icy notes.*
    Prince LI CHIN

*Home-sent letters,*
*Home-wending dreams,*
*Between them lies*
*Gaping Eternity.*
*An empty bed*
*And Autumn sere*
*Vie with each other*
*On the score of desolation.*
*The green moss*
*Below the steps,*
*The red trees*
*In the courtyard,*
*Now mope*
*In the rain,*
*Now melt into Sorrow*
*In the moonlight.*
    LI SHANG-YIN

*The splendid glories of the past*
*Have been pulverized into fragrant dust.*
    TU MU

*The roads are long, but my dreams are short.*
    LU KWEI-MENG

*This city once rode upon the floating clouds,*
*And vanished into the emerald of evening.*
*Now again it accompanies the setting sun,*
*Splashing the echoes of Autumn.*
*There are countless painters in the world,*
*But who can paint this patch of poignant pathos?*
    K'AO CH'AN

Ay, who can paint this patch of poignant pathos? This is the "inscape" of Winter, and painters can only paint landscapes. Who can paint a glimmer of light amidst a choir of crickets, or the maple leaves being dyed to crimson by lingering thoughts, or the wind scattering green sorrows among the ripples, or a little garret being frozen out and out by the icy notes of a jade pipe, or dead hope buried in a bloomless bud, or the green moss and red trees moping in the rain and melting into Sorrow in the moonlight, or the splendid glories of the past pulverized into fragrant dust? And above all, who can paint the dreams? And yet there is a subtle seductiveness about all those lines which somehow grapples your heart to them more tightly than any "hoops of steel." They are like pomegranates opening to the night, staining the darkness with their dusk-etherized tints. The tints are not faint in themselves, but they are fainting in the circumambient oblivion.

We may say of the winter poetry what Li Shang-yin says of the pear-blossom:

> It phosphoresces in the moonless night.
> It forces itself to smile when a storm is
> brewing in the sky.

What tenderness lies impanate in these lines! Our hearts would be broken, if Shakespeare had not assured us:

> The robb'd that smiles steals something from the thief.

And Li Shang-yin's description of a dying girl seems to fit Winter like a glove:

> Her forlorn soul is flickering out in the maze of life.
> Her gossamer breath is gasping charmingly away.

The whole output of the belated songsters in the last days of T'ang reminds me of a beautiful line by Wen T'ing-yün:

> The apricot-flowers fall incense-breathing to the ground.

In trying to define the indefinable qualities of Winter, I feel like one suffering from the itch. The more I scratch, the more itchy I feel. Perhaps, Winter can best be studied in relation to the other seasons. In appearance it can be as gay and blithe as Spring. Listen to Prince Li Yu's song, "Let Us Enjoy":

> To welcome Spring, one must come before Spring.
> To enjoy the flowers, one must not wait till they are withering.
> When such soft ivory hands offer a cup of effervescent wine,
> Who has the hardness of heart to decline?

*Why not beam in smiles alway?*
*In this Forbidden Park, Spring finds a cosy place to stay.*
*Let us drink our fill and talk ad libitum!*
*As for poetry, I find a rhyme in every beat of the drum!*

And yet one cannot help feeling that we have here only a Dionysian in garment, Spring in a minor key. It seems to me that Verlaine knows the mind of Prince Yu:

*Your soul is a sealed garden, and there go*
*With masque and bergamasque fair companies*
*Playing on lutes and dancing and as though*
*Sad under their fantastic fripperies.*

*Though they in minor keys go carolling*
*Of love the conqueror and of live boon*
*They seem to doubt the happiness they sing*
*And the song melts into the light of the moon.*

Prince Li Yu is no more springlike at heart than Thomas Hardy:

*Let me enjoy the earth no less*
*Because the all-enacting might*
*That fashioned forth its loveliness*
*Had other aims than my delight.*

We have already pointed out that Winter is as angry as Summer, but not as outspoken. Its satires are more subtle and more pregnant. Tu Fu says:

*Behind the red-painted doors, wine turns sour and meat stinks:*
*On the roads lie corpses of people frozen to death.*
*A hair-breadth divides opulence and dire penury!*
*This strange contrast fills me with unutterable anguish.*

But Tu Mu would say:

*In this world only the white hair is just and fair,*
*For it does not spare even the heads of the great!*

A very naughty friend of mine has given a modernized version of it:

*In this world only the white hair*
*Is just and fair:*
*For it does not spare*
*Even the head of a millionaire!*

Tu Fu asks openly:

> *When will the war cease and farmers return to their fields?*
> *And when will the petty officials cease to fleece the poor?*

But Ts'ao Yeh deals out a somewhat more subtle blow:

> *In the public granaries,*
> *The rats have grown*
> *Almost as big as a cow.*
> *They don't run away*
> *When they see men*
> *Come near them.*
>
> *The soldiers at the front,*
> *Their food-supplies are running short,*
> *And the people are starving.*
> *Nowadays,*
> *The grain is meant*
> *Only to fatten the rats!*

Tu Fu wants "to turn his majesty into a greater man than Yao and Shun," the sage emperors of old; but Nieh Yi-chung only wishes the heart of the sovereign to be transformed into candlelight:

### THE POOR FARMERS

> *In March they sell out their new silk.*
> *In June they place new grain on the mart.*
> *'Tis like dressing the wounds of the skin*
> *With slices of flesh torn from the heart!*
> *I wish the heart of the Sovereign*
> *Would soon a bright candlelight become,*
> *To shine not on a splendid feast,*
> *But on a runaway's drear home!*

If, as Somerest Maugham says, Michelangelo is the father of baroque, in the same sense we may regard Tu Fu as the father of the later T'angs. Just as Tu Mu is called "the little Tu," so we can call Winter "the little Summer." I think that at heart Winter is more affiliated with Summer than with the other seasons. Is this not the reason why men like Sinburne and Pater were so greatly attracted by Victor Hugo?

Winter is as desolate as Autumn, but its desolation has acquired colors and got a body. The pangs of regret become "red," and sorrows become "green." Dolors are transmuted into colors. Desolation seems to beat on like a live heart that has been segregated from the poor mortal whose heart it used to be. Here is what Li Shang-yin sings about the lady in the moon:

> I sit behind the screens of marble
> In front of a shaded candlelight.
> I have watched the Milky Way
> Gradually going down,
> And the morning stars sinking.
>
> Ah, you Lady in the Moon!
> How you must have repented
> Your theft of the Elixir of Life,
> For which you have been condemned to live eternally,
> With your heart bleeding from night to night
> In the loneliness of the murky sea and the blue sky!

The following poem by a contemporary poetess, Yeh Ching-i (1879–1926), seems to be as wintry as Winter can be:

### A FAREWELL TO SPRING

> The wailing cuckoo has called the Spring away.
> Desolation is blowing in the wind!
> Desolation is dripping in the rain!
> Desolation is filling the air with the flying flowers!
> The flower of Time is fading before my eyes.
> Sadness rings in the nightingale's song!
> Sadness echoes in the swallow's twitter!
> Sadness lingers on, when the Spring is gone!

Indeed, to pass from Autumn to Winter is like watching pensive evening deepening into night. I have made a parody of John Gay to reveal what I mean:

> Life is a jest, and all things show it:
> Autumn thought so, but Winter knows it.

To sum up, then, Winter is Spring in a minor key, Summer under cover, Autumn in gloss of satin and glimmer of pearls. But has it got a soul of its own? Has its soul died beyond the possibility of revival? My answer is that, with most of the winter poets, the soul is only lost in the maddening maze of things, but not actually dead. And deep down in the heart there lurks a mystical censer, which has acquired a spark of life from its very antiquity, and which sends forth intermittently invisible wisps of incense in search of the soul it once possessed. These ethereal wisps rise like silent somnolent prayers to God, whose heart is easily melted by the aroma of green thoughts and red fancies.

# THE WINTER
# OF T'ANG POETRY

*The melancholy notes of the birds are floating on the eventide.*
SZU-K'UNG TU

*Trailing along a dying echo,*
*The cicada flits into a neighboring bough.*
FANG KAN

*The day is at its sunset,*
*The year is in its wrecks.*

TSUI TU

*Look in my face; my name is Might-Have-Been;*
*I am also called No-more, Too-late, Farewell.*
G. C. DANTE ROSSETTI

*Wandering between two worlds, one dead,*
*The other powerless to be born,*
*With nowhere yet to lay my head,*
*Like them, on earth I wait forlorn.*
MATTHEW ARNOLD

AROUND 840 TU MU wrote a poem to a Taoist priest who was by that time nearly a centenarian:

*Pale and emaciated, you have lived almost a hundred years.*
*To the weather-beaten temple another Spring has come.*
*The whole world has long since become a battlefield:*
*You alone of our contemporaries were born in the days of peace.*

The fact is that ever since the rebellion of An Lu-shan in 755, the T'ang Dynasty had not known a single day of peace. Nor was there the slightest ray of hope for the restoration of the body politic to anything like its normal health. On the contrary, things were moving from bad to worse; and more than a century was to elapse before China was united again under a new regime, namely, the Sung Dynasty, which established itself in 960. During that long period, with the exception of twelve years (from 847 to 858, in which a series of victories were effected against some of the bordering tribes, and there was a brief breathing space and a faint promise of a renaissance), the country was writhing under all sorts of evil, such as intrigues of the eunuchs, brigandage, uprisings, massacres, mutinies, party squabbles, foreign invasions, rebellions of the warlords, famines and plagues. At the wake of the fall of the T'ang Dynasty in 906 China was split into a host of little dominions, like a flower-pot shattered into shards. Among those little states, the Southern T'ang, which was established in 937 with Nanking as its capital and was to last till 975, is of special interest to us. For in the first place, its founder was a descendant of T'ang; and secondly, a formidable group of poets, including Princes Li Chin and Li Yu, flourished in it. It may therefore he regarded, in poetry as well as in politics, as the afterglow of the T'ang Dynasty.

In short, the Winter of T'ang poetry covers a period of about one hundred and forty years, that is, from 840 to 978, the latter being the year in which Prince Li Yu died.

There is, of course, no hard and fast line of demarcation between the seasons, especially between Autumn and Winter, as both belong to the shady side of the year. But there is no more appropriate date than 840 to mark the beginning of Winter. It was the year in which the poor Emperor Wen Tsung died from neurasthenia. Shortly before his death, chafing under the oppression of the eunuchs, he suffered a nervous breakdown. Sometimes he was found standing waywardly and gazing blankly before him; at other times, he was found muttering and sighing to himself. On one occasion he summoned a minister before him and asked him, "Of all the emperors of the past, with whom do you think I can compare?" The minister answered, "Your majesty belongs to the company of Yao and Shun!" But his majesty did not think so. "How dare I aspire to be Yao and Shun?" he said. "The reason why I asked you is whether I am not inferior to Chow Nan and Han Hsien." The minister was taken aback, and asked, "They were good-for-nothing monarchs at whose hands their respective dynasties were wrecked and finished. How can they compare with your majesty?" "But don't you see," Wen Tsung rejoined, "that they were only oppressed by powerful dukes, while I am held in grip by my own family slaves? From this standpoint, I am even worse than they."

There can be no better illustration of the wintry mood than this. An impotent fury conscious of its impotence, a feeling that the end has come, a pang of regret that finds no words but issues in sighing and whimpering to oneself, a loss of self-confidence, a defeatist attitude toward life, a sense of responsibility for the miseries of the world which one has in no way caused and can in no way remedy, a realization that only a miracle can save the world from another deluge and that there are no miracles, an increase of sensitiveness coupled with a failure of nerve, a drowning man's quickened recapitulation of all his past experiences—these are some of the symptoms of the spirit or rather spiritlessness of the age whose poetry we are now to survey.

Wen Tsung was the author of the well-known poem:

> On the roads grows the Spring grass.
> In the park the trees are flowering.
> I lean upon a high balcony, musing alone.
> Who knows the infinite pathos in my mind?

All nature is blossoming forth, but the heart is shut up within itself like a dead fetus rotting in the womb. This poem sets the tone to the poetry of Winter.

Let me first present a group of poems, which forms a composite picture of Winter both in its external and internal aspects.

### SULLENNESS

> Dim, dim the waters of the long river.
> Faint, faint the heart of a far wanderer.
> The fallen flowers seem to loathe one another,
> They drop to the ground without a sound.
>
> Ts'ui Tao-yung

## SPRING

*A forlorn man in the green Spring,*
*How I hate to see the flowers!*
*On the roads I meet a group of drunken fops,*
*All wearing garlands on their heads.*

Ts'ui Tao-yung

## SENDING CLOTHES TO THE SOLDIERS

*A battle was raging at night*
*Amidst a heavy snowfall.*
*The soldiers from the interior,*
*Half of them were killed.*
*In the morning came letters from their homes,*
*Together with the clothes made by their wives.*

Hsu Hun

## THE RURAL CONDITIONS

*I walk alone among the wild fields.*
*I see the doors of the farm-houses all closed up.*
*I ask where the farmers have gone.*
*I am told they have all gone into business.*
*The government does not tax the traders,*
*But only taxes the toil-ridden farmers.*
*So they leave their farms and travel east and west*
*On the roads that lie contiguous to the dikes.*
*Some have gone into the mountains to quarry jade;*
*Others are diving into the seas to get pearls.*
*But the soldiers at the frontiers want food and clothing;*
*To them jade and pearls are as good as soil and mud.*
*In the old days, the labor of one farmer*
*Could barely furnish food to three mouths.*
*Now out of thousands of families*
*Not a single person holds the plough and hoe.*
*Our granaries are constantly empty,*
*Our fields are overgrown with thorns and briars.*
*Heaven does not rain grains of rice.*
*How can we keep the teeming masses from starvation?*

Yao Ho

## A WINTER NIGHT IN THE HILLS

*The leaves fall,*
*And shiver in the cold wind.*
*Only a few birds*
*Nestle in the bare trees.*
*The brooks are frozen,*
*And the deer are thirsty.*
*The snows on the hills prevent*
*The return of the monks.*
*Sitting up in the night,*
*My heart is purged of dust.*
*Humming my verses,*
*My voice grows faint.*
*Enough of loafing!*
*But where is my home?*

CHANG CH'IAO

## THE BORDER TROUBLES

*On the northern frontiers the clouds of war are looming,*
*And our Imperial Government is raising troops again.*
*Sullen blasts rage more fiercely toward the evening;*
*The killing breath of Autumn is making havoc of the land.*
*The trees being destroyed, birds are nestling in the grass.*
*The ice thickening, people are walking on the rivers.*
*Since there is no Kuo Tsu-i today,*
*How can we expect the barbarians to sue for peace?*

LI CH'ANG-FU

## WAILING

*In the glimmering lamplight*
*My beard looks black.*
*The green grass mopes*
*In the shade of gloomy walls.*
*The year coming to an end,*
*I bewail the world and myself.*
*All of us are glow-worms,*
*In the grip of the frost.*

SZE-K'UNG TU

## AUTUMN THOUGHTS

*A sick body living in a perilous age,*
*How often have I fainted from weeping in Autumn!*
*Blasts and billows are raging and heaving;*
*Heaven and earth are turning flip-flap.*
*An orphan-like glow-worm flits on a waste land;*
*Falling leaves pierce through a shattered house.*
*The world is getting more snobbish than ever;*
*Who will call upon a solitary castaway?*

SZE-K'UNG TU

## ARE WE IN A CUL-DE-SAC?

*The sun and the moon*
*Journey on without cease*
*Day and night.*
*They bring to men*
*Now prosperity,*
*Now decay.*
*The righteous ones*
*Are not always*
*On the wane,*
*Nor will the wicked*
*Remain always*
*Full and bright.*
*God is impartial;*
*'Tis man who stumbles*
*And incurs calamities*
*By his own wrongs.*
*Fickle and inconstant,*
*He goes astray from God*
*I wish the great Creator*
*Will hold the wild beasts*
*At bay;*
*Fill the seas*
*With precious things,*
*And the earth*
*With flowers and willows;*
*And separate once for all*
*The evil and ugly*
*From the good and beautiful.*

*Then people's hearts*
*Will return to Simplicity,*
*And the wars*
*Will cease for ever.*

Su Cheng

## PARTING FROM A FRIEND AT AN INN

*The day is at its sunset,*
*The year is in its wrecks.*
*Illness forbids me*
*To hope for much new;*
*Age sharpens the pain*
*Of parting from old friends*
*The mountains have come to an end,*
*But the roads are still rugged.*
*The rain has stopped,*
*But the Spring is as cold as ever.*
*How can I bear to look back?*
*Where the beacons burn is Ch'angan!*

Ts'ui Tu

## AT NANKING

*The rain is pouring incessantly on the river,*
*Grass is growing thickly on the banks.*
*The Six Dynasties have vanished like a dream;*
*The birds' cries sound hollow.*
*The most heartless are the willows along the wall:*
*They still sway carelessly in the midst of smoke and mist.*

Wei Chuang

## A GIRL'S YEARNING FOR HER LOVE

*I took out the mirror*
*From the hibiscus case,*
*But I have no heart*
*To look into it.*
*My waist was slender*
*Enough as it was,*
*But I find my gauze girdle*
*Growing looser than ever.*

*Ever since you left home,*
*I have not played the flute;*
*For my thoughts are as cold as its notes,*
*Which you alone can warm up.*
*My heart yearns*
*To see you in dreamland.*
*But the roads are long,*
*And my dreams are short.*
*Angry with my fate I sit up*
*Bewailing the west wind.*
*The autumn window is filled*
*With the bright beams of the moon.*

P'I JIH-HSIU

## LINES WRITTEN ON A NEW YEAR'S DAY

*From month to month,*
*I look about the same.*
*From year to year,*
*I look differently.*
*This morning, as I peeped*
*Into the antique mirror,*
*I found the features of one*
*Wrecked by years of traveling.*
*In the bustle of the world,*
*Quiet leisure is hard to get;*
*And what one is forced to do*
*Is mostly much-ado-about-nothing.*
*My floating life will not last*
*Much longer anyway.*
*'Tis time to get drunk*
*With the winy breath of Spring.*

HSU T'ANG

## BOATING ON THE RIVER

*The great river holds the city of Chang in its embrace.*
*Facing the Isle of Parrots live families of staggering wealth.*
*Some rich fops are sleeping in their painted boats.*
*In their dreams, they are transformed into butterflies*
*    hunting after the flowers!*

YU HSUAN-CHI

## THINKING OF HIM

*I hate you, O water of Chin Huai!*
*I hate you, O boats on the river!*
*Years ago you bore him away from me.*
*But when, O when will you bring him back to me?*

*That year when he took leave of me,*
*He said he was going to Tung-lu.*
*Now I don't see the man from Tung-lu,*
*But get a letter from Kwangchow!*

*Yesterday was happier than today.*
*This year is older than last year.*
*The turgid Yellow River may some day turn clear:*
*But blackness will never return to the white hair.*

LIU TS'AI-CHUN

## THE NUPTIAL NIGHT

*The waiting maid, coming to remove the cosmetic box,*
*Was surprised to find the bride already in bed.*
*But really she had not slept.*
*She was sobbing furtively with her face turned away.*
*Languorously she took down the phoenix hairpin.*
*Blushingly she slipped into the nuptial quilts.*
*From time to time she espied the corn-like candle, burned almost to*
*  its end,*
*Dropping down its golden ear together with smoke.*

HAN WU

## LOVE

*Lingering, lingering,*
*Pulsating, pulsating,*
*Two hearts beat in one.*
*Fine as gossamer,*
*Vast as the waves,*
*Inconstant as the moon,*
*Frail as a flower,*
*This strange thing we call love,*
*What a prolific source of sorrow it is!*

WU YUNG

## WAITING FOR A FRIEND AT NIGHT

*The bright moon is setting.*
*The autumn wind is growing chill.*
*Is he coming tonight, or is he not?*
*The shadow of the wut'ung tree is fading out:*
*But here I'm standing still!*

LU T'UNG-PING

## A SATIRE

*How elaborate the beautiful lady's coiffure!*
*What lovely pearls and emerald jades on her head!*
*Does she realize that the two specks of cloud she wears*
*Wear out the taxes of several villages?*

CHEN YUN-SOU

## A POOR GIRL

*A poor girl, I have never tasted*
*The perfumed robes of precious gauze.*
*I try to find a good match-maker,*
*But what is the use?*
*Who in this world would appreciate*
*High romance and pure love?*
*Who will ever marry a girl*
*Without the attraction of a dowry?*
*All that I have to offer*
*Is the skill of my fingers.*
*I have not even the heart to paint*
*My eyebrows in appealing arches.*
*Year in, year out, how I groan*
*Under the endless heaps of golden threads!*
*Ah me! When shall I cease to make*
*The wedding dresses of other girls?*

CHIN T'AO-YU

## THE SILKMAIDS

*Morning and night*
*They gather the mulberry leaves.*
*Patiently they toil and moil.*
*Even in the season of bright flowers*

*They find no time to enjoy themselves.*
*If they too know how to follow*
*The frivolous fashions of the world,*
*The fashionable ladies*
*Of the golden houses*
*Would be frozen to death.*
                              LAI KU

## BUTTERFLIES AND SWALLOWS

*When the flowers bloom,*
*Butterflies cluster around them.*
*When the flowers wither,*
*Butterflies take leave of them.*
*Only the swallows*
*Return to their old nests*
*In spite of the poverty*
*That has befallen their host.*
                              WU KUAN

## ON THE WRITING OF POETRY

*Don't talk of the craft of poetry!*
*No other craft is so full of difficulties.*
*Before you can put a single word in the right place,*
*Your moustache will be thinned out by constant twirling.*
*The exploration for what is new and uncommon*
*Would wear out the patience of Heaven.*
*The fastidious search for the exquisite and precious*
*Would exhaust the resources of the ocean.*
*For poetry is not like prose*
*Which admits of prepositional makeshifts.*
                              LU YEN-SUN

From these specimens the reader will find one thing about the winter poets: Whenever they are not weeping, they are flirting. The preoccupation with sex is always a symptom of low vitality. Winter is lustful where Spring is lusty. It is only when one's libido is dying out that one would brag as Baudelaire does:

*My spirit, you move with a pure ardency,*
*And as one who swoons in the senses of sound,*

> *You furrow furiously the immensity profound*
> *With an invincible and male sensuality.*

Another thing to note is that the language of the poems of this period (I mean of course the original) is refined to the point of agony. When great poetry is dead, people begin to produce light verses and to write poems on poetry. The whole movement of the T'ang poetry began as a revolt against rhetoric: it ended as a cult of rhetoric. The style of the Six Dynasties has come back again. This is a concrete illustration of Samuel Butler's insight: the history of art is the history of revivals.

Having presented the general atmosphere and features of the age, we are prepared to treat some of the better known poets individually. There is a plethora of poets during the 9th Century; but I confine myself here to the big three: Tu Mu, Wen T'ing-yun, and Li Shang-yin.

Tu Mu (803–852) was one of those poets who, disappointed with life, sought refuge in wine, women, and song. He wrote a caricature of himself:

> *A lost soul amidst rivers and lakes,*
> *I never travel without bringing wine along.*
>
> *Ah, the charm of the slender-waists, so light and slim*
> *That they could almost dance on my palm!*
>
> *Waking from a dream of ten years in Yangchow,*
> *I find myself famous as a heartless fop!*

But he was really not so heartless as he was reputed. Here is a touching farewell song he wrote to one of his girls:

> *True love looks like no love.*
> *I only feel I cannot smile before the cup.*
> *Even the wax-candle has a heart and pities our parting,—*
> *It drops silent tears for us until the dawn!*

It seems as though he was too sad to weep and had to borrow tears from the candle. He had too much love for his poor heart to contain.

Of all the girls in the Green Chambers of Yangchow, he seems to have taken a special fancy to one:

> *A maid just o'er thirteen,*
> *So graceful and so arch!*
> *A nutmeg bursting into leaf*
> *In the early days of March!*

*In the streets of Yangchow,*
*Aquiver with the breath of Spring,*
*All the pearl-screens are rolled up,*
*But I see none so ravishing!*

I suspect that it was the same girl whom he saw fourteen years later. At that time she was already married and mother of quite a few children. He wrote a symbolic poem, which touches a note of deep pathos:

## SIGHING OVER A FLOWER

*Oh! How I hate myself for coming so late*
*In search of the flower!*
*Years ago, I saw her before she had blown,—*
*Just a budlet was she!*
*Now I find the wind has made havoc of her,—*
*Her petals strew the ground!*
*I only see a tree with a thick leafage*
*And branches full of fruits!*

Not all his poems deal with love; but whatever he sings is charged with wintry forlornness and expressed in a style which has some funereal sleekness about it. A few specimens will suffice:

## AT AN IMPERIAL CEMETERY

*The pale boundless space has swallowed*
*The faint shadow of a lonely bird.*
*Ah, this is where all the ages of the past*
*Have been drowned and dissolved into nothing!*
*What has remained of the glories of the Han Dynasty?*
*Only the bare Imperial Tombs swept by the Autumn wind!*

## THE GARDEN OF GODDEN VALLEY

*The splendid glories of the past*
*Have been pulverized into fragrant dust.*
*The stream flows on indifferently,*
*And the grass keeps Spring to itself.*
*At sunset, the singing birds*
*Lament the passing away of the East Wind.*
*The falling flowers recall the pretty one*
*Who threw herself from a high balcony.*

## A NIGHT AT AN INN

*A cold lamplight evokes memories of the past.*
*The broken notes of the wild geese pierce through my sorrow-ridden*
   *sleep.*
*My home-wending dreams impinge upon the dawn.*
*The letters from home cross the boundary of years.*

## ROAMING IN A MOUNTAIN

*Driving up the cold mountain*
*Along the coils of a rocky path,*
*I find in the depth of the white clouds*
*Several families are leading a quiet life.*
*I halt my carriage and sit awhile*
*To admire the maples in the eventide.*
*How the frost has dyed their leaves*
*To a deeper crimson than the flowers of March!*

Wen T'ing-yun (820–880) was another hermit of the Green Cham-bers. Once he met at an inn Emperor Hsuan Tsung, who was traveling incognito. The emperor asked him, "Do you know who I am?" Wen answered, "I think you are a bodyguard of the emperor." The emperor never forgave him for that, and Wen was doomed to remain out of office.

Reading his poems makes one feel as though one were in a jeweller's or a draper's shop. Feminine pulchritude is his main concern. The fol-lowing four pieces will suffice to illustrate his style:

## TO A SINGSING BIRD

*A secluded lane meanders alongside the river.*
*A little door is on the latch all day.*
*The crimson pearls grow on the curtains like ripe cherries.*
*The gold-tailed peacocks stand idly on the marble screens.*
*Her tresses of cloud enchant the butterflies with their fragrant smell.*
*The yellow patches on her temples remind one of twilit hills.*
*You and I can remain an inseparable pair of golden ducks!*
*Let us forget the lures of the outside world!*

## A WEARY NIGHT

*The fragrant breath of the jade censer*
*And the crimson tears of the wax-candle*
*Fill the Painted Hall with autumnal thoughts.*

*The emerald on her eyebrows is paling.*
*The cloud on her temples is fading.*
*The night is long, and the quilt and pillow cold.*

*The wut'ung tree,*
*The midnight train,*
*They don't know the pang of nostalgia.*
*Leaf after leaf,*
*Drop after drop,*
*On the empty steps they fall till the dawn.*


## A NOCTURNE

*The clear sky*
*Hangs like a mirror*
*Upon the hook-like moon.*

*The endless ripples of the river*
*Glint sorrows*
*Into the traveler's heart.*

*Nocturnal tears*
*Ooze furtively*
*From the Song of Bamboo Springs.*

*The distant echoes*
*Of the Spring Tide are flooding*
*My little boat of spice wood.*

*Events pass away*
*Together with the clouds,*
*Leaving our bodies behind.*

*Our dreams dissolve*
*Like wisps of smoke;*
*The waters flow on.*

*Where are the joys of yesterday?*
*A plum-tree has shed its blossoms into the river.*

A SPRING DAY

*In the south garden,*
*The ground is strewn*
*With piles of light catkins.*

*In sorrow I listen*
*To the sudden showers*
*Of early Spring.*

*After the showers*
*Comes the evenglow;*
*The apricot-flowers fall*
*Incense-breathing to the ground.*

*Silently I smooth*
*My sleep-ridden face,*
*As I lie on my pillow*
*Behind the screens.*

*The twilight is closing in upon me;*
*I stand wearily leaning against the door.*

Li Shang-yin (813–858) was not a hermit of the Green Chambers, but he had secret affairs with the nuns in the Taoist convents and with the maids-of-honor in the imperial harems. A considerable number of his poems deal with those adventures of love, and are couched in a language which is as obscure as it is beautiful. No poet has a greater mastery of the mysterious suggestions which lie concealed in words. This is how he writes:

*From my room I gaze despairingly*
*Into the fathomless dusk.*
*A flight of jade stairs lies across the sky,*
*Severed from the hook of the moon.*
*The banana tree refuses to unfold its leaves;*
*The clove remains a closed bud for ever.*
*Each nurses a private sorrow in its bosom,*
*Though both breathe the same Spring air.*

One does not know exactly what the flight of jade stairs is; and yet the lines inevitably convey the idea of an unbridgeable gulf between the lovers. And who can ever forget such lines as:

*The silkworm in the Spring goes on*
*Spinning gossamer threads until its death.*
*The wax-candle ceases not to weep*
*Its tears of blood until it burns itself to ashes.*

*The stars of yesternight!*
*The wind of yesternight!*
*West of the Painted Hall!*
*East of the Cinnamon Hall*
*Our bodies possess no wings*
*Like those of the gorgeous Phoenixes.*
*But our hearts commune with each other*
*As those of the mystical Rhinoceros.*
                        \*   \*   \*   \*   \*

*When heaven is desolate,*
*And the earth withers,*
*You will feel your heart rent apart.*
*But the pain is not half as intense*
*As when Spring mocks you*
*With all its rich splendors!*

No one is so perfectly winterlike, in sentiment as well as in style, as Li
Shang-yin. The following are some of his representative poems:

### GETTING UP IN THE MORNING

*A breezy, dewy, mild and clear morning.*
*Behind the curtains, a lonely man is getting up.*
*The orioles wail, but the flowers smile.*
*Which of them, I wonder, is the real Spring?*

### SPRING

*The breeze of Spring is kind enough at heart:*
*But the things of Spring grow too exuberantly.*
*If Spring were a thoughtful lover,*
*He should have concentrated all his love upon a single flower.*
*My mind is different from the mind of Spring:*
*My heart is broken even before the coming of the flowering season!*

### SORROW IN SPRING

*Everyday the Spring is racing*
*With the rays of the sun.*

*The apricot flowers fill*
*The suburbs with their perfume.*
*Ah me! When will my heart*
*Be freed from the grip of sorrow,*
*So it can grow as long as the gossamer*
*And waft carelessly in the air without breaking?*

## WINTER

*The sun rose on the east,*
*The sun has set in the west,*
*The lady Phoenix flies alone,*
*The female Dragon has become a widow.*
*Frozen walls and hoary-headed frosts*
*Join in weaving gloom and sending doom*
*To the flowers, whose tender roots are snapped asunder,*
*And whose fragrant souls have breathed their last!*
*The wax candles weep tears of blood*
*Lamenting the coming of the dawn.*

## THE EVEN GLOW

*Feeling fretful in the eventide,*
*I take a drive and mount the ancient plain.*
*How infinitely charming is the setting sun!*
*Only it is so near the yellow dusk.*

## FAR FROM HOME

*Spring finds me far from home,*
*Far from home, and near the sunset.*
*If the wailing nightingale has tears,*
*Let her wet the topmost flower.*

## SENT TO HOME

*You ask when I shall come home.*
*There is no date yet.*
*Just now, here at Pa-shan,*
*Night rain is flooding the Autumn pools.*
*I look forward to the time*
*When we shall snuff the candle*
*Together by the western window.*

*And I shall tell you how I feel*
*This night at Pa-shan,*
*When the rain is flooding the Autumn pools.*

## THE FALLEN FLOWERS

*On the high pavilion,*
*Revels have ended and guests gone.*
*In the little garden,*
*Flowers are flying in disarray.*
*They cover up*
*All the meandering paths.*
*They form a long parade*
*To send off the glorious sunset.*
*My bowels have snapped asunder.*
*I have no heart to sweep away the scattered petals.*
*The more I strain my eyes,*
*The fewer flowers remain on the trees.*
*Their fragrant soul has given up*
*Its last breath with the Spring.*
*And what remains?*
*Only tears that bedew my raiment.*

## THE LADY IN THE MOON

*I sit behind the screens of marble*
*In front of a glimmering candlelight.*
*I have watched the Milky Way*
*Gradually going down,*
*And the morning stars sinking.*
*Ah, you Lady in the Moon!*
*How you must have repented*
*Your theft of the Elixir of Life,*
*For which you are condemned to live eternally,*
*With your heart bleeding from night to night*
*In the loneliness of the sea and the sky!*

## THE YO YANG TOWER

*To disperse the pent-up sorrows of a lifetime,*
*I have mounted the Yo Yang Tower on the Tung T'ing Lake.*
*How I wish to ride on the endless waves to the bourne of Heaven!*

*Only the sinister dragons are too much bent upon the overturning of
boats.*

## TO THE WILLOWS IN AUTUMN

*How you used to sway in the east wind,
Brushing gracefully the pretty dancers!
Now the Spring Garden is turned into
A scene of broken hearts!*

*Why have you lived to see
The days of pale Autumn,
To pine away in the fading sun,
Amidst the dirge of cicadas?*

## VISITING A MONK

*The last beams of the sun
Have sunk behind the western hills.
I have come to the thatched hut
To call on the solitary monk.
Fallen leaves all around!
But the man is nowhere to be found.
Now the coiling path that has led me up here
Is enveloped in the chilly clouds.
All alone, I beat the stone-chime
To sound the knell of the day.
Attuned to the universal stillness,
I lean quietly upon a twig of rattan.
The world is contained in a little speck of dust.
There is no room for love and hate.*

In connection with the last quoted poem, I wish to introduce a comparison of the seasons. Solitude is always an attractive theme for the
poets, irrespective of ages and countries. But how one feels when in
solitude is what makes the difference. Li Shang-yin could not have felt
as the Spring poets did:

## A NIGHT AT THE PEAK TEMPLE

*I stop the night at the temple on the Peak.
Stretching out my hand I feel the pulse of the stars.*

*I dare not make any noise,*
*For fear of startling the folks in Heaven.*

Li Po

## AT A TEMPLE

*In the clear morning I stroll into an old temple.*
*The tall trees are radiant with the first beams of the sun.*
*A coiling path leads me into a secluded spot.*
*The Dhyana Hall is hidden in the depth of flowers and trees.*
*The clear light of the mountains delights the nature of the birds.*
*The crystal face of the pond cleanses the heart of man.*
*All the discordant notes of the world are mute.*
*One only hears the serene music of the bell and the stone-chime.*

Chang Chien

Nor could these Spring poets have sung as Tu Fu did:

## A NIGHT AT THE LUNG-MENG TEMPLE

*After guiding me in the excursions of the day,*
*The head monk invites me to spend a night at his temple.*
*The dark ravine oozes with the music of silence.*
*The moonlight casts the clear shadows of the trees.*
*Between the cliffs hangs a scroll of throbbing stars.*
*Sleeping among the clouds, my clothes are drenched.*
*The morning bell has caught me on the point of waking;*
*Stirring me into a violent searching of the heart.*

But this searching of the heart is a little too violent for an autumnal spirit like Po Chü-i:

## AT THE HSIEN YU TEMPLE

*A crane has come over from the sandy beach*
*And stands quietly on the steps.*
*The moon blooms like a flower*
*In the pond in front of the door.*
*There is something around here*
*That makes me feel at home.*
*After spending two nights,*
*I still feel like staying on.*

*I am glad to have chanced upon this secluded place,*
*With no companion to hasten my return.*
*Now that I have tasted the joy of solitude,*
*I shall never come here in a company.*

# LI YU:
# THE PRINCE OF WINTER

*Winds wander, and dews drip earthward;*
  *Rain falls, suns rise and set,*
*Earth whirls, and all but to prosper*
  *A poor little violet.*

I. R. LOWELL

*Spring flowers and Autumn moon—how long is the pageant of*
  *seasons to last?*

Prince LI YU

*Pile the pyre, like the fire—there is fuel enough and to spare; . . .*
*Burn the old year—it is dead, and dead, and done.*

SYDNEY DOBELL

IF I AM ASKED who is the greatest poet of China, I would say Tu Fu. But if I am asked what poet is dearest to my heart, I would say Prince Li Yu.

Prince Li Yu acted in his own person a tragedy that only Shakespeare could have written, and his lyrics are comparable to the soliloquies of Hamlet and Lear. Some of his best lyrics, at any rate, come so directly from the heart and are clothed in such perfect language that if Shakespeare were to write a tragedy of his life in Chinese, he would certainly have adopted them verbatim. I have no heart to deal with his life in detail. It is too sad a story to tell. But his poetry is so bound up with his life that a few pivotal facts must be given here.

He was born in 936. In the following year his grandfather established the Southern T'ang, covering a territory of about a thousand square miles on the south of the Yangtze River, and with Nanking as its capital. He assumed the title of an emperor. From the beginning it was a weak state, surrounded by more powerful neighbours. The star of the Sung Dynasty was steadily rising, and the poor Southern T'ang was just like the morning star soon to be outshone by a greater light.

In 943, the grandfather died and Li Yu's father, Li Chin, ascended the throne. During his reign, it was no longer possible to maintain the title of an emperor in his relations with other states, so he assumed the title of a king. He was a poet of no mean order, and has two exquisite little pieces to his credit:

## AN EVENING IN SPRING

*I have rolled up the pearl-screen.*
*But the Sorrow of Spring,*
*Like a bird inured to its cage,*
*Refuses to fly out of the window.*
*The flowers are falling in the wind,*
*Like guests taking leave*
*Of a world without a host.*
*My thoughts lengthen to eternity.*
*No fairy birds have brought to me*
*Any message from beyond the clouds.*
*My heart is like the clove*
*That has shrivelled in the rain*
*Into a bloomless bud, in which dead Hope*
*Lies entombed in its very womb.*
*Turning my head backwards,*
*I see green waves rolling and billowing*
*Through the dusk-shrouded land of Ch'u*
*Towards the azure sky.*

## A GIRL THINKING OF HER LOVE

*The fragrance is faded from the lotus-flowers,*
*And the emerald leaves have withered.*
*The west wind is scattering sorrows among the green ripples.*
*Everything seems to be decaying with my years,—*
*I cannot bear the sight.*

*Interwoven with the silken rain,*
*My dreams are hovering round the remote Border of Cock-crow.*
*All alone I have been blowing the pipe of jade*
*Until my little garret freezes out and out with its icy notes.*
*With endless sorrows flowing in endless pearly tears,*
*I lean silently on my balcony.*

In 961 when Li Yu was twenty-six, his father died, and he ascended the throne. By that time, the Southern T'ang was already a vassal state of Sung. The founder of the Sung Dynasty summoned him several times to his capital, Kaifeng, Honan; but he persistently declined to go on plea of ill-health. Getting impatient, the Emperor sent his troops down to attack Nanking in 974. The city was surrounded for a whole year before it was surrendered. Li Yu was brought to the capital, and spent his last two years in captivity as the "Marquis of Recalcitrancy." In a letter to his former maids-of-honor, he said, "Here in exile, I wash my face with my tears day and night."

In the night of the Double Seven in 978, Li Yu celebrated his birthday with wine, women, and song. The next day he was poisoned by the reigning Emperor.

Li Yu was one of the most affectionate men who have ever worn a crown. He was an affectionate son, brother, husband, father, friend, and monarch. Even before his captivity, there were more tears than smiles in his life, for the little tragedies of life affected him more profoundly than they would a less poetic nature. For instance, there is a very touching poem in memory of his wife and son:

> *A sad memory clings to me eternally.*
> *A secret pain gnaws at my heart.*
> *The rain deepens the loneliness of Autumn,*
> *Sorrow aggravates my sickness.*
> *Standing to the wind, I gulp down my sobbing thoughts.*
> *Blear-eyed, I seem to see flowers in the air.*
> *O Lord of Death! Hast thou forgotten me?*
> *Thy shiftless son is weary of wandering.*

I am tempted to call him "the weeping king." He wanted always to remit death sentences, but his ministers remonstrated against his over-leniency, and he yielded to them weeping. He wept so much for his subjects that they could not help weeping for him when they heard of his tragic death.

His poetry may be divided into two periods: before and after captivity. Naturally, the poems of the second period are more touching; but those of the first are nonetheless fine pieces of art. Here are some specimens:

## THE FISHERMAN'S SONGS

*The foam of the waves simulates endless drifts of snow.*
*The peach-trees and pear-trees silently form a battalion of Spring.*
*A bottle of wine,*
*An angling line,*
*How many men share the happiness that's mine?*

*An oar of Spring wind playing about a leaf of a boat.*
*A tiny hook at the end of a silken cord.*
*An islet of flowers,*
*A jugful of wine,*
*Over the boundless waves liberty is mine.*

## TRYSTING SONGS

*Her bronze pipe emits a crisp tune like that of cool bamboo.*
*She plays a new air with her ivory fingers moving gracefully.*
*She entices me furtively with her eyes,*
*Overwhelming me with their charming waves.*
*Clouds and showers in a secluded anteroom!*
*Whenever she comes, my heart sings like a melody.*
*But the feast is soon over, and the rest is silence.*
*My soul is lost in the cobwebs of spring dreams.*

*She has just finished her evening coiffure,*
*Sprinkling herself with a little sandal scent.*
*She sings a sweet tune,*
*Slightly revealing her clove-like tongue,*
*Which softly wedges her cherry mouth apart.*
*The gauze sleeves are enamelled with ruby floods,*
*A deep cup is filled with the fragrant dregs of wine.*
*Leaning languorously on the embroidered pillow—Ah, what an*
    *image of tender grace!*
*Chewing a fragment of red wool to pulp,*
*She spits it out, smiling demurely at her sweetheart.*

The flowers are scintillating in the dim moonlight.
A light fog suffuses the air.
'Tis an ideal night to go to my love!
In socks I walk tip-top over the fragrant steps,
With a pair of embroidered shoes dangling from my hand.
I meet my love in a cozy corner south of the Painted Hall,
And throw myself trembling into his embrace.
" 'Tis so hard for me to steal out:
Taste me to the full!"

## A GIRL'S YEARNING

One range of mountains,
Two ranges of mountains.
The mountains are far, the sky high, the mists and waters cold.
My lingering thoughts have reddened the maple-leaves.
The chrysanthemums bloom,
The chrysanthemums wither.
The wild geese from the border fly high, but my love has not come
    home.
The wind and the moon play idly on the screen.

## THE REVELS ARE OVER

The cherries have fallen, and Spring has returned to Heaven.
The pair of light-powdered butterflies is frolicking in the air.
The nightingale is wailing the moon west of my little chamber.
The gauze curtain hangs gloomily from a jade peg,
Brooding in the mists of the twilight.
The guests have gone, leaving a little mansion in utter loneliness.
There remains only the dreary grass as a relic of happier days.
Wreaths of frankincense rise silently and linger around the stone
    Phoenix.
I find myself holding listlessly a silken girdle in my hand,
With my heart full of lingering regrets.

## AGAIN

The flowing days of Autumn, they will not remain.
The steps are strewn with the scarlet leaves, the year is on the wane.
Ah, the Double Nine has come again.
And the arbors on the high plain
Are filled with the perfume of the dogwood again.

*The breath of the purple chrysanthemum*
*Is wafting in the courtyard lane.*
*The evening smoke hovers enshared in the silken rain.*
*In the cold air the wild geese faintly complain.*
*The same old sorrow and the same old pain!*

## THINKING OF MY LOVE

*A tress of cloud!*
*A shuttle of jade!*
*A pale, pale robe of thin, thin gauze!*
*A nameless grace playing about her knitted brows*
*Like a faint shade!*
*Autumn gales start,*
*Echoed by the rain.*
*Outside the window screen*
*A pair of plantain-trees grow wide apart,*
*The long, long night wears out a longing heart.*

## A QUIET NIGHT

*A mansion secluded and quiet,—*
*Serenity dwells in the little courtyard.*
*Intermittent sounds of the cold anvil and pestle in the intermittent*
*  gales.*
*How they keep me awake during the long, long night,—*
*These solitary notes wafted on the moonlight into the screened*
*  window!*

If these and such as these were all he has done, he would still have a place in the history of Chinese literature as a *petit maitre*. But it was in his days of exile that he produced the poems that have endeared him to the hearts of all his readers and made him the Prince of Winter. The following are some of his best known:

## REMINISCENCE

*A country with a history of forty years,*
*Possessing thousands of li of mountains and rivers,*
*With Phoenix Pavilion and Dragon Tower towering to the skies!*
*Dodders of jade with beautiful sprigs of precious gems,—*
*  that was all I saw.*

*How many times did I ever see the weapons of war?*
*One day I became a captive slave.*
*My graceful waist and delicate features have wasted away.*
*Ah, I can never forget that day when, after I had taken leave of*
    *my family temple,*
*The Academy of Music played a doleful song of farewell,*
*And I wiped my tears in front of the maids-of-honor.*

## TEARS, ENDLESS TEARS!

*Tears, endless tears!*
*How they soak my sleeves and trickle on my chin!*
*Ah, let not your sorrow-laden heart drop with your tears!*
*Ah, blow not the Phoenix-pipe in tears!*
*Else your heart is sure to break or burst!*

## A DREAM

*Ah, how sad!*
*Last night in my dream*
*I was again roaming in the Royal Park*
*Like in the old days—*
*Carriages were rolling like a stream*
*And horses prancing like dragons—*
*Moonlight flowers were quivering*
*In the warm caress of the Spring breeze!*

## UPON WAKING FROM A DREAM

*Outside the window-screen the rain drizzles and drips.*
*The Spring is gasping away.*
*Under thin silken quilts I shiver in the cold tide of the morning*
    *watch.*
*In a dream, forgetting my homeless plight,*
*I feasted myself like a glutton upon the past joys again!*
*Ah, lean not upon the balcony all alone,*
*Lest you should see the endless rivers and mountains,*
*That make separation so easy and meeting so hard!*
*The stream flows on, the flowers have fallen and the Spring is*
    *gone,*
*Leaving no trace in Heaven or on earth.*

## LIFE IS A DREAM

*In life no one is wholly immune from sorrows and griefs.*
*But who ever felt as I do now?*
*In my dreams I return to my fatherland:*
*Upon waking a pair of tears drop from my eyes.*
*With whom can I go up the storeyed mansion now?*
*I only remember how beautiful the fair days of Autumn used to be.*
*Past events have vanished without leaving a trace behind.*
*They are no more than a dream.*


## HOME THOUGHTS IN SPRING

*My idle daydreams carry me to the southern lands,*
*Where fragrant Spring is in full bloom.*
*In the boats pipes and strings make riotous music, and the face of*
    *the river is green.*
*The catkins mingled with the light dust, are flying pell-mell in the*
    *whole city.*
*The sight-seers in the flowery gardens are busied to death.*


## HOME THOUGHTS IN AUTUMN

*My idle daydreams carry me far.*
*I see quiet, pellucid Autumn in the southern lands.*
*A thousand li of rivers and hills drenched in cool twilight.*
*In a thicket of rushes is moored a solitary boat.*
*The mellifluous notes of a flute come from a moon-lit tower.*


## HOMESICKNESS

*Since we parted, Spring is half gone,*
*Every sight breaks my heart.*
*Below the steps the plum-blossoms fall in confusion with the*
    *flakes of snow.*
*They are no sooner brushed away than they cover me over again.*
*The wild geese bring no news from home.*
*The roads are long, but my dreams are short.*
*Homesickness is like the grass in Spring:*
*The farther you travel, the thicker it grows.*

## PARTING SORROW

*Speechless I am up here alone in the Western chamber.*
*The moon is like a sickle.*
*In utter loneliness the limpid Autumn is locked within a secluded*
   *mansion by the paulownia trees.*
*Scissors cannot cut,*
*Nor combs comb,—*
*That's parting-sorrow.*
*It has a taste of its own that's known to the heart alone.*


## 'TIS FATE

*Vernal redness is faded from the flowers.*
*Ah, why so soon?*
*But who could prevent the cold showers in the morning and*
   *the cruel blasts in the evening?*
*How the tears, dyed in the rouge*
*Used to coax me to take more wine!*
*When will this happen again?*
*'Tis as inevitable for life to overflow in sorrows as for*
   *the waters to flow the east.*


## A SLEEPLESS NIGHT

*Last night rains came in company with the gales.*
*The latticed curtain echoed the Voice of Autumn.*
*The candle flickered, the water clock stopped, and many times*
   *I leaned upon the pillow,*
*And tossed in my bed and sat up restlessly.*
*The events of the world forever follow the flowing stream.*
*What is life but a floating dream?*
*In the Drunken Land alone are the roads even and smooth.*
*In no other lands can I walk without stumbling.*


## LONELINESS

*What a pain 'tis to remember the joys of yesterday!*
*In my present plight, how they mock to prey!*
*The Spirit of Autumn haunts the courtyard, and mosses overgrow*
   *the pathway.*
*A row of pearl-screens hangs idly and motionless like a painted wall.*

*Who comes to call throughout the day?*
*My golden sword is buried away.*
*My youthful dreams wither and decay.*
*This evening, the weather is cool, the sky clear, and the blooming*
*   moon is in its full display.*
*Ah, fancy that at this very hour the jade towers and crystal domes*
*   are casting their silent shadows*
*Upon the lonely waters of the Chin Huai!*

## NOSTALGIA

*Upon the window beats the rain.*
*Spring is on the wane.*
*My silken quilt is too thin the pre-dawn chill to sustain.*
*In a dream, forgetting that I am a stranger in a strange land,*
*I slipped into the happy old days again.*
*Ah, lean not wistfully upon the windowpane!*
*Hills and rivers form an endless chain,*
*Which makes separation so real and yearning for home so vain.*
*The stream flows on, the flowers are falling, and the Spring is*
*   going—*
*Between heaven and earth yawns the boundless inane!*

## HIS LAST POEM

*Spring flowers and Autumn moon!*
*How long is the pageant of seasons to last?*
*Who can remember the endless events of the past?*
*My little chamber was astir again with the breath of the east*
*   wind last night.*
*Ah, how could I bear to think of my vanished country in the bright*
*   moonlight?*
*Carved balustrades and marble stairs must still be there:*
*Only faces cannot always be fair!*
*How much sadness, you ask, can be harbored in my breast!*
*Even as the swollen rivers in spring rolling eastward without*
*   a moment's rest!*

The seasons of T'ang poetry have come to an end. A new year is beginning!

I can find no fitter conclusion for this long article than a poem by the springlike poet, Chang Chiu-ling:

## AN ALLEGORY

*In Spring, how lush the leaves of the orchid!*
*In Autumn, how pure the flowers of the cinnamon!*
*All things are quickened by the same breath of life:*
*But each has a blooming season of its own.*
*Who knows the hermits among the woods?*
*How they attune their moods to the changing winds!*
*The grass and trees grow from an inner urge,—*
*Not for the sake of being plucked by pretty hands!*

# INDEX